# A Practical Guide to Enq
# Primary Teachir.g

This book is a guide for developing an enquiry approach in primary schools and offers practical ideas on how to empower teachers to embrace spontaneity and flexibility in their daily practice.

Designed as a thinking diary, this book provides space for the practitioner to record highs and lows in the classroom and experiences in meetings and training, ensuring it serves as a personal record of what works well but also a pertinent reminder of what can improve and what can be learnt from mistakes. *A Practical Guide to Enquiry-Based Primary Teaching* comprehensively covers all the steps involved in adopting this approach, including:

- why enquiry-based learning should be at the forefront of primary settings;

- how to develop teachers in this approach and assessing the prior learning which needs to take place beforehand;

- settling into your role as a facilitator and recognising the strengths and weaknesses within your enquiry team;

- discussing and planning enquiry sessions, including clarifying objectives;

- how to let go of a more structured approach to learning and becoming familiar with the tools in your spontaneity arsenal;

- evaluating enquiry sessions.

Supported by research, this book is a fresh, innovative approach to enquiry-based learning and teaching and will be a valuable daily aid for both newly qualified and experienced primary teachers.

**Helena Hill** has over twenty years' experience as a primary school teacher. She currently teaches Reception at Warren Wood Primary, where she has been the Foundation Stage Leader for the past three years and is also a member of the Senior Management Team.

# A Practical Guide to Enquiry-Based Primary Teaching

## A Reflective Journey

## Helena Hill

Routledge
Taylor & Francis Group

LONDON AND NEW YORK

First published 2019
by Routledge
2 Park Square, Milton Park, Abingdon, Oxon OX14 4RN

and by Routledge
711 Third Avenue, New York, NY 10017

*Routledge is an imprint of the Taylor & Francis Group, an informa business*

*British Library Cataloguing-in-Publication Data*
A catalogue record for this book is available from the British Library

*Library of Congress Cataloging-in-Publication Data*
Names: Hill, Helena, 1969- author.
Title: A practical guide to enquiry-based primary teaching: a reflective
journey/Helena Hill.
Description: Abingdon, Oxon; New York, NY: Routledge, 2019.
Identifiers: LCCN 2018025952 (print) | LCCN 2018032792 (ebook) |
ISBN 9780429487675 (ebook) | ISBN 9781138596306 (hardback) |
ISBN 9781138596320 (pbk.) | ISBN 9780429487675 (ebk.)
Subjects: LCSH: Primary school teaching–Great Britain. |
Inquiry-based learning–Great Britain.
Classification: LCC LB1556.7.G7 (ebook) |
LCC LB1556.7.G7 H55 2019 (print) | DDC 372.1102–dc23
LC record available at https://lccn.loc.gov/2018025952

ISBN: 978-1-138-59630-6 (hbk)
ISBN: 978-1-138-59632-0 (pbk)
ISBN: 978-0-429-48767-5 (ebk)

Typeset in Celeste and Optima
by Deanta Global Publishing Services, Chennai, India

# Contents

# Contents

# Figures

# Preface

Use this book as a practical guide towards developing an enquiry approach in primary schools. It is a thinking diary to improve your skills in being a spontaneous teacher and leader of enquiry and developing a climate where if there's something you don't know, then together we'll work it out. Where the process of finding out will be far more rewarding and deep rooted in the learning process, becoming a way that you learn rather than something you know.

Leaders of enquiry should use this book to challenge how their school teaches and as a professional development tool, supporting the school's development planning. The thinking diary-style layout will become a personal and bespoke journal.

In a culture of believing that knowledge is the be all and end all, the notion of implementing an enquiry approach has difficulties. The process of how we learn being given more importance than an end product is why an enquiry approach is essential. Think of those times when children's learning has been exciting; you remember those moments when the hairs stand up on the back of your neck as you witness a 'wow' moment! This becomes long-lasting learning, when children 'get' something and don't just acquire a fact.

This book will help you develop an enquiry approach in your teaching and your school. Use it as a thinking diary by adding your own experiences and questions and, along with your school, begin the amazing journey of letting go and promoting a learning environment of collaboration, creativity and reflection.

An enquiry approach in schools requires teachers to become practised in letting go and being spontaneous. This book will give you practical ideas on how to empower teachers to build on their experiences, encouraging teachers to want to have a go at enquiry teaching whilst giving them confidence. It will challenge the negative view of 'winging it' and allow them to see that it is a skill which needs fostering and nurturing just like any other skill.

# Acknowledgements

Thank you

To the editorial staff at Routledge, Bruce Roberts and Alice Gray, for believing in this idea.

To Lynda Trueman and the inspiring people at Early Excellence.

To my family and friends, especially Stephen, Phoebe and Ruby, for coming on this enquiry journey with me; your excitement and love has kept me motivated to do the best I can.

To my Mum (Anne Newton) for being my cheerleader!

To my teaching friends for pushing me every day to think about teaching and learning and for making my job so much fun.

To Erica for being my best friend and inspiring me to do this; I am so pleased we got a second chance.

# All aboard

We want our children to be free-thinking, independent learners; yet the system they are educated in can be rigid and straightjacketing, not promoting the values in education that we crave for our children.

Is the ideal of a creative and free environment where children explore, ask questions, explain to each other and have fun obtainable? Is it possible to reach a high level of independent learning in an atmosphere of performance, targets and timetabling?

Furthermore, can we teach openly and feel less guilt? Organisation and planning have dangerously overtaken an honest and spontaneous approach to teaching and learning.

In a culture of believing knowledge is the be all and end all, the notion of implementing an enquiry approach has many difficulties. There are substantial gaps between how schools are being asked to deliver the curriculum, how learning is being encouraged around the world and how teachers perceive how education works. The process of learning being given more importance than the end product is why an enquiry approach is essential. In my own experience, those times when children's learning has been exciting and long lasting is when they are working hard to explore and hang on to those life-changing moments when children 'get' something, as opposed to remembering a fact or method that has little intrinsic meaning at that moment in time or for the future.

Do you remember the organisation of many 1970s junior classrooms? If not, then lucky you! It was row upon row of wooden desks with a lift-up lid, pencil sharpener shavings stuck to the bottom with ink splats. If we talked we were shouted at and we had to fill exercise books with sums. Handwriting featured *a lot*, with endless practising and copying. Art lessons were a favourite of mine but looking back we all did the same thing; there was no responsibility for creating or developing your own ideas. We used to do a project at the end of term and I must have done two or three scrapbooks about France.

1

I loved it there and wanted to express my thoughts with drawings of the flag, map and the Eiffel Tower. However, all the scrapbooks were identical. Why was this never challenged? Why was I not encouraged to try something new? Why were my stereotypical drawings of French people unchallenged?

Thinking back, and remembering, praise was given to those who achieved academically. Later, some of the teachers from my school were very surprised that I had become a teacher because I struggled a lot, especially with reading. I just didn't get it. Reading Comprehension was a total mystery to me and the scheme we used was fiddly, with little vocabulary cards that fitted into slots to form sentences. It just didn't do it for me. I didn't really enjoy reading until I was pregnant and on maternity leave with lots of time to spare (as my first born was late!). At that time I read and read and now enjoy reading about teaching and learning, so that it is a skill that has been a slow burn for me.

Not everyone is the same and I'd like to think that if I was at school now, teachers wouldn't allow me to do the same repetitive tasks. Instead they would challenge me and support and inspire me to feel confident in my abilities and to take responsibility for my learning. Looking back I never really had those 'wow' moments. I was happy and have fond memories of the Infant school where subjects seemed to merge and rooms were dedicated to different subjects, so that we had a reading and writing room, and an art room and we were free to roam from one to the other, but still not in a challenging or enquiring style. I think we want more for our children today.

Therefore, in this guide you will find achievable goals to develop an enquiry-style curriculum and learning policy for your school. Use this guide as a learning journal by adding your own experiences and questions; along with your school, you will begin the amazing journey of letting go and promoting a learning environment where if there's something you don't know then, together, we'll work it out. Even if there's no right or wrong answer, the process of finding that out will be far more rewarding and deeply rooted in the learning process, becoming a way that we think rather than something we know.

The idea of this journal is to follow the learning path with your school; include all staff, children and parents in presenting your school's way of learning. By developing the responsibility of the staff to allow children to make decisions and try something new, parents will have the assurance that they are sending them to a positive, forward-thinking school that endeavours to provide the best learning environment possible.

Enquiry can take on different forms. Ultimately you want enquiry to weave through the curriculum and timetable, but you may need to organise off timetable days or 'wow' days to generate enthusiasm and impact, as well as to give a platform for staff and children to practise enquiry skills in an organised way. Once everyone feels confident and totally values the process, it can roll out into everyday practice and you can start to form the group of teachers that I am going to call Team Enquiry.

At the beginning of an enquiry or on an off-timetable 'wow' day, use the learning path to give structure to the learning taking place. It is a misunderstanding that enquiry means no structure. A straightforward framework is essential to give teachers the confidence to have a go at a new style of teaching where responsibility and ownership are handed over to the learner and is not dictated by the teacher.

Teachers are not now the primary resource of knowledge for children, so our role now has to be that of a guide, opening up possibilities and allowing children to take risks, be creative and develop their critical thinking skills. This approach can cause anxiety for many, so buckle up your belt for a bumpy road! This journal will help teachers to feel in control and captains of their own destiny rather than feeling out of control and watching the lesson unravel before their eyes, or remain static and uninspiring.

Maintaining the balance is what this journal will help you to do, as well as to explore the ways in which you learn, collaborate with others and prepare children to develop their skills as a learner, now and in the future. The future for children in education is unknown so we need to prepare for the pathways children can take as learners into the future.

In using this guide successfully, you have to have flexibility and confidence in yourself in responding to new ideas and the ideas of others. If someone's response to a new initiative is "well, we've always done it like this", then their starting point is very different from someone who says, "show me how it works, I'll have a go". The art of embedding enquiry positively is in establishing enquiry procedures and practices which fit generally with the majority view, yet allow everyone to explore their understanding and skill set. We learn most when we are at the edge of our comfort zone, so be clear about this at the start. You are going to ask teachers to possibly change and do something they feel uncomfortable with. Reassure them that we will do this together and the whole teaching team should provide a supportive atmosphere where strengths are celebrated and weaknesses supported.

Be open about your practice and how things work. Some see this as a weakness but if you want to influence change, let them see how you do it – by sharing ideas as a commonplace routine and letting them 'pinch' your practice ideas. Establishing this sharing atmosphere will open up the key to good practice and take away the competitive nature within teams that performance is a solitary status that teachers are on their own doing the same things in the same way and being protective of how they think it works best. Teachers *are* creative beings and given the right environment where collaboration and raw enthusiasm is built upon and given a purpose, amazing things will happen with enquiry.

It will take time to get everybody on board and things at times will get messy. Regularly remind staff and yourself that you're not asking to get rid of all their previous ideas. Mistakes will happen along the way, but together when learning is opened up and practice is put under the microscope, real meaningful change with no 'finger pointing' can take place.

One of my favourite books is 'Show your work by Austin Kleon. It has nothing to do with schools but everything to do with sharing your creativity and collaboration. He says that "when you share knowledge ... you receive an education in return" (Kleon 2014: 119). Setting the scene in your school of a sharing community could be the hardest thing you do but, equally, the most rewarding and it will ultimately benefit the learning environment in school. Once you start this process, gaps will appear and those gaps will become your starting point. For me, it was ensuring that everyone understood the power of enquiry, seeing the value of a whole school theme or off-timetable day and setting up learning opportunities rather than disseminating knowledge and a curriculum that's been done in the same way for a long time to pupils. These are hefty starting points but at least I knew where to start and where to go!

You need to find your starting point. It might be that elements of enquiry are already being used in your school, so build on them. Knowing the context of your school will be very important in finding your way. Consider both staff confidence and children's experiences to start your enquiry school. It could be that many children have valuable experiences out of school, though they are not given the freedom to explore independently. They may have a wealth of ideas but lack the reflective skills in order to learn from mistakes. There are no judgements here, just a fact-finding mission to find your starting point. Equally, interact with the staff to work out what teaching styles are generally going on and gauge their willingness to try something new at a meaningful level.

This can take time and it could become a drip-feed effect which actually, though it may take years to implement rather than months, does become embedded more strongly as opposed to a quick 'wham, bam' initiative that might seem very exciting but lacks the substance and longevity that enquiry has. These small interactions that you have with teachers and children will all add up to building an enquiry school and you need to acknowledge them and celebrate them. I get such satisfaction from listening to snippets of conversations about what has worked well in a class or how certain children have progressed from year to year. I like to think I've played a part in promoting that recognition of learning and opening up thinking throughout the school.

Use the reflection page to explore your starting point (Figure 1.1).

**Figure 1.1** Reflection page

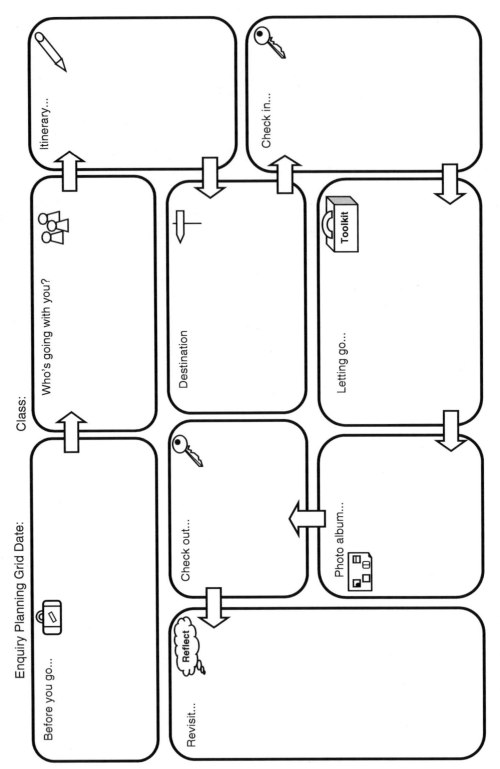

**Figure 1.2** Planning grid

Figure 1.2 is the planning grid; this is the template to use for enquiry planning. Each section of this book will help you to add to the plans to give structure and direction to your enquiry pathway personally and as a school. It will, hopefully, help you to plan for every eventuality and guide you through implementing an enquiry approach.

Someone asked me at school if I wanted the school to use this grid through the planning stages for everything. Wouldn't that be amazing! I answered that yes, the ultimate aim would be that, but we're not quite there yet. We've got a lot of work to do before this is in place.

This book will follow the planning grid as you implement an enquiry style and promote an enquiry ethos with all.

It flows along your journey from finding your personal starting point to recognising the areas for development in others and creating a structure to planning and delivering enquiry. There will be lots of opportunities along the way to make your own notes and reflections, so use them to bring clarity and purpose to your journey.

# 2

# Before you go

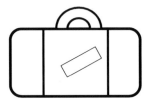

**Figure 2.1**

Confidence goes a long way in bringing others on board, and however experienced you are it's essential to have a clear understanding of your strengths. I have been in many staff meetings when teachers have delivered a message apologetically and with a "well, I'm not going to do it but I want you to do it" mentality. This will get you nowhere fast. It's not about appearing like a 'know it all', which I've felt from others several times, and which may cause some to disappear and mumble to each other about what you've said. It's more about establishing your role, being positive and being confident in your ideas so that your enquiry teaching spreads and sneaks up on people and becomes absorbed into learning and teaching.

Before you go on this enquiry journey, it's important to think about your role in the school. This obviously could be quite varied, as some may be established teachers, newly qualified or a phase leader. You may feel that it's not your responsibility to promote enquiry in your wider school or that it's not your job. Have faith that whatever your position, an enquiry school is the future and you will be an integral part of its functioning.

If you are new to the school, I appreciate that it is difficult to have the courage to say your bit. However, if you can make those small changes or have a go at some of the ideas in this guide then you will start to build the enquiry building blocks. You might get noticed for being a teacher who is willing to have a go. Remember that you aren't carrying the same baggage as some others, so what have you got to lose? You might end up leading this area or supporting another teacher, so collaboratively your role in school will become more established.

This guide can be used to lead your own learning with your class. Trial the activities from each platform and discuss them with a mentor or critical friend. You could end up being the pathfinder for enquiry in your school. Being new to teaching or joining a school as a newbie can be exhausting. You have to get your head round all the new policies and procedures as well as to get to grips with behaviours, learning objectives, marking policies and – on top of everything – relationships with children, parents and other teachers.

It's a lot to take in so I can appreciate that enquiry might not be at the top of your list. However, if you can crack this, your teaching will become a lot more purposeful and your relationships will be much more supportive. Being an effective teacher depends on you growing as a person, listening to others, collaborating, making mistakes and reflecting on them. You need the opportunity to offload and empty your mind so that you can develop (and sleep!).

Teachers work really hard – they often get to school early and don't leave until late, and then they take work home with them – so make this hard work count and be smart about it. Enquiry underpins all curriculum subjects, learning characteristics and behaviours – it underpins everything. I actually think it should be a priority for all teachers. So establish the pathway for enquiry in this guide, whether you're young, old, newly qualified, on teaching practice or a curriculum leader. You may even be a mentor to a recently qualified teacher. Support them and shape them into being enquiry teachers so that they are part of the inspirational group of teachers that are going to be known as Team Enquiry. You never know, it might encourage you to join in and practise your enquiry skills. That openness to change and a willingness to try new things will be valuable characteristics in a time when education is changing and curiosity, enquiry and creativity are desired qualities in our teachers and learners.

Now is the time to really think hard with your staff about what you really want your curriculum to look like and, more importantly, how you want your children to learn! You want to get away from the production line approach of "this is what we do, this is when we do it and this is what the children *will* learn". Take this opportunity to revamp how you approach learning for yourself and for the staff and seize the moment in exploring the possibilities of pushing enquiry forward so that it becomes how you learn, not what you learn.

Watch the Sir Ken Robinson (2010) clip called 'Changing education paradigms'; it will really make you think about how we can make changes to teaching and have a huge impact on the learning experiences of our children.

If you are an enquiry leader, use it in a staff meeting to spark a discussion about your school's ethos.

Before the school knows it, they've got a bespoke curriculum, motivated students and confident teachers. This obviously takes time, but you'd be surprised how quickly this ethos does grow once everyone realises that the characteristics of learning are the foundations for achievement. Being that person who never gives up and keeps going, adapting, reflecting and re-evaluating influences change. This positivity permeates through everything and it's impossible to resist.

Be very clear about what an enquiry teacher is! You will find a few ideas in Figure 2.2.

This is a great starting point for you. Some of these characteristics will apply to you and teachers that you're working with. You may have other traits that you think are just as important. Create your own personal Wanted poster (Figure 2.3).

What are your qualities as a teacher and leader of learning? Take some time to reflect on your qualities and give examples of things you've done which celebrate your strengths.

You now need to do this with your fellow teachers if you are leading enquiry. Slot it into a staff meeting time. Even established teachers need a reminder of what makes them tick and why they entered the profession.

I remember drawing my imaginary school and putting all the words inside that I thought represented me as a leader of learning. You might already know but seeing it written down in text or drawn as a picture can reaffirm your principles and qualities when you feel you are losing your way or not being listened to. Refer back to this page in order to give you the oomph to carry on.

Once you've had an amazing enquiry experience it's hard to go back. It's different for everyone, you'll have your own personal journey and so will everyone else and this becomes addictive as you become flushed with the success of the students. These moments, when the hair stands up on the back of your neck as you witness a 'wow' moment or a child that is just so happy to be 'in the moment', are what will keep your drive going.

So, hopefully you're feeling ready to take on the challenge. You need to put 'enquiry' into the visioning of the school and your teaching. You can't be an island and do this on your own, so push forward your willingness to lead this area. Discuss what skills you want the students to develop through enquiry. This is the perfect way to start everybody's thinking about enquiry teaching. Flip it onto its head by asking: what do we want our students to be like? What do we want them to remember about our school? How do we want them to learn?

# WANTED

**Are you...?**

spontaneous

flexible

ambitious

gritty

determined

confident

good communicator

listener

Figure 2.2

Figure 2.3

This discussion will give you a real insight into what the current thinking is in school and what everyone desires for their students. If you are a new teacher, then what a great start to finding out about the ethos of the school. If you are an enquiry leader then this will give you a learning agenda to refer to regularly in meetings and training sessions. Refer back to the words that the staff generated and use them as a measure within the curriculum and in procedures in the school so that they weave into every day.

When I delivered this visionary meeting, after a great deal of discussion many words were decided on – 'celebration', 'flexibility', 'open-ended', 'communication' and 'creativity' were the main ones suggested. You can't argue with any of that and these and more skills will benefit the learning behaviours of everyone. Have a similar discussion with your staff and gather the characteristics they hold dear for their school. These words can be displayed in school and can become part of your learning policy.

Once this has been established in your role, it's now time to turn your thoughts to the staff and school team. There will be many colleagues eager and willing to take an enquiry approach on board and you really need to bond with these people. You should establish a positive dialogue with these teachers and spark ideas off each other. Give them responsibility, 'go' with their ideas and support them in brainstorming their ideas into reality.

Understanding the dynamics of the team you are working with is essential. The group (hopefully) of teachers that are like-minded will become your backbone in pushing forwards. They are the energetic, respected and open-minded teachers that you need to embed an enquiry approach; so encourage them, get them on-side and talk to them about what's working well and what made that particular lesson so great. Establish a professional dialogue and write down what they say. You are one of this group too, so exchange ideas, thoughts and concerns and help each other to overcome hurdles. Be a mentor role for each other. This group of teachers is Team Enquiry and you will need them along the course of your enquiry journey.

It is also important to gauge reactions from the children too and to find out what motivates them. What are their views of their school and what made them eager to come to the school? You could use this knowledge if you are in Early Years to promote your school to feeder pre-schools and nurseries and show them ... 'What our children say about our school' leaflets or posters. It should be reflected in the teaching and learning policy in your school. If you are a newly or recently qualified teacher, a student on placement or just new to the school, it's your job to make sure you are using these words in the classroom and that you are giving children plenty of opportunities to practise them.

You also need to find out what is motivating them right now, so early on use pupil voice sessions to canvass pupils' opinions about favourite programmes, games, toys, etc. What's the current trend? Some things are recurring trends year on year, such as bikes, the park or swimming, and some are more specific to advertising campaigns or television programmes. Use the reflection page to gather current trends (Figure 2.4).

Once you have this knowledge, use it in your classroom and planning. Incorporate it into your reward system.

You can take this further by sending discussion questions home and asking children and parents what things they would like to find out about. I did this with one year group and lots of replies came back; there was one that stood out, as the girl had researched pirates in her free time. She had started her own research and brought in photos, so we decided to go with that and she was so happy. At that moment we had caught her imagination and motivation to learn. We'll talk more about motivation later.

This needs to be an exciting fact-finding mission and something older children can organise themselves. They could design the letter to go home and also give you a current insight into their cultural references. Don't be too hung up about how they are going to explore the ideas; just get them buzzing and excited.

Use the reflection page and note possible questionnaire ideas to send home (Figure 2.5).

Working with younger children makes it easy to capture imaginations – 4- and 5-year-olds can get excited about frozen peas! Children know what they like, so tap into their experiences.

Families will have their favourite topics too, whether they are generated from films, books or the outdoors, so canvassing their opinion will give value and responsibility.

Planning needs to be fluid and adaptable; for this reason, the best way to start is by having nothing other than a few ideas and then from that using parts of schemes or handbooks to give more structure.

It is important to have a skill-based curriculum for foundation subjects and then to see how subjects can interlink to create a loose programme of work. English will fit in with this style of planning perfectly, although mathematics needs more attention, so maybe keep that planning separate for now. You need to be following the skills.

Once you have a theme or topic, choose broad topic titles. Water, for example, is easier to plan for. Superheroes may seem very exciting but can be quite constraining. Use objects or photographs as a stimulus for discussion with the children. What do they know? What do they want to know?

With these discussion ideas, go back to your team and find common ideas and plan out the most interesting questions to be explored. There are lots of examples of 'What do I know?' formats out there – get using them (Figure 2.6).

**Figure 2.4** Reflection page

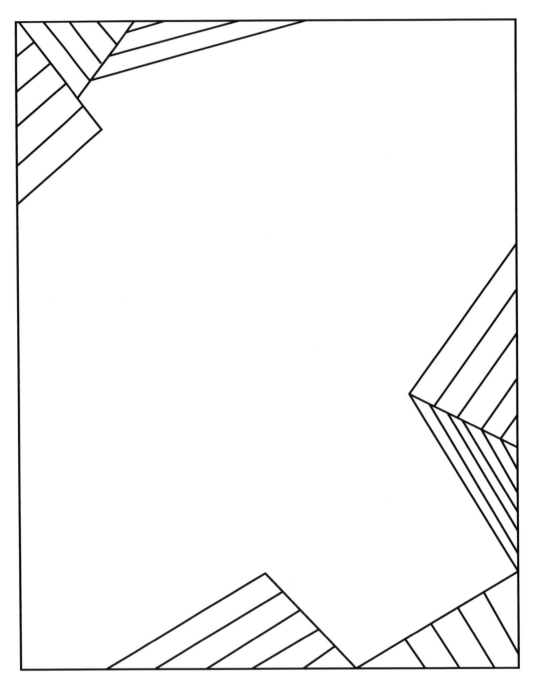

**Figure 2.5** Reflection page

| What do I know? | What do I want to find out? |
| --- | --- |
|  |  |

**Figure 2.6**

The planning grid needs to be a constant to help maintain the flow of the enquiry session as well as to appeal to those teachers and children who prefer a structure.

I like a good plan that settles me and gives me a foundation to bounce off. Going off at a tangent is fine but knowing the ultimate goal gives me the confidence to continue. This plan does that.

In this section of the learning path you need to consider the prior learning of the children. What do they need to know before starting the enquiry? Maybe they need to know some basic facts around the subject, for example geographical features, vocabulary or names of famous scientists. The children definitely need to know how to ask questions, what they already know and what they want to find out.

Are your children aware of what a question is? With younger children it can give you hours of fun, yet often children lose this habit as they grow older. Which is strange, because very young children ask 'why?' all the time? Maybe they've been given the message from an early age that when they ask "... but why?" and we roll our eyes they realise that it's annoying and give up, or may we give them the answers too quickly, so they don't take responsibility of the thinking part to the answer. In Reception I spend a lot of time establishing what a question is; that early curiosity seems to have been lost.

Right from the outset resources and classrooms should promote exploration, curiosity and enquiry. Therefore, check out the Continuous Provision in your Early Years setting and ask yourself ... does it stimulate enquiry? Look at other classrooms throughout the school – is there an atmosphere of curiosity in the room? Do the rooms have open-ended resources for children to explore? Are there displays about Growth Mindset, examples of questions and prompts to enquire?

You may need to do some work with your staff purely on questioning. Use the reflection page (Figure 2.7) to explore your understanding and the school's

**Figure 2.7**  Reflection page

understanding of open-ended questions and why they are important. Most teachers will have knowledge of different types of questions and how they give more opportunities for children to shine and make links and patterns to further deepen their understanding. Know that there may not be a right or wrong answer but make them aware of their approach. Try to allow children to see patterns:

"Have you done something similar before?"

"Do you think it will happen this time?"

"Why?"

Make questioning a habit and a tool to regulate your own learning:

"How do you know you're right?"

"Can you explain why?"

This builds confidence to explain and reflect on experiences and should be quickly established in the enquiry process. Children who can make links between their own experiences and future outcomes as well as see the bigger picture and reflect on it with confidence will become adept at enquiry.

## Home links

An easy way to include parents at this stage is to invite them in to take part in the question session. Use photographs or objects as a stimulus and ask parents to take their children around the objects. The children could write questions on Post-its, or describe what they know about the stimulus. This is a useful way of gauging the questioning skills and descriptive language of your pupils, but also helps parents to see how their children work with other children, how they talk to each other and how the teacher manages the several conversations happening all at once.

Parents often see the end result – for example. the painting, information book or assembly. They don't necessarily see the questioning, planning or process. There can be too much emphasis on the end result, so give parents the opportunity to see the process before the final piece. It could take the form of an 'open day'-type session, or research questions done at home for a future enquiry.

Simultaneously, it can be chaotic on the first go but exciting for the children, welcoming for the parents and informative for teachers. The questions generated during this session will give the structure to the enquiry. The children can then decide which questions they want to answer.

Before you start an enquiry, it is important to be in control of the equipment you are likely to use. Is IT going to be an issue? Do you need to book the laptops or other devices for your class and are they working?

Sometimes, you may want a speaker or knowledgeable person to introduce the enquiry. Check they can be available or book the expert. A 'hands-on' practical activity is a good way to build interest and motivation. Dressing-up days are a good way to start an enquiry; just make sure everyone knows – staff, children and parents. Maybe a family has been on holiday to the place you are enquiring about – bring them in to be the holiday guide or rep.

Think about how you are going to group the children during the day.

Some children may need to be grouped in a certain way due to needs or qualities. However, try to mix them regularly as you still need them to be flexible when collaborating. It might be that you want to give certain children the opportunity to present, as this is a strength and you want to celebrate it. Or you want a different child to practise making links in patterns and change that builds their confidence. It is worth spending time with your team, discussing the different characters in your school and how best to support them in getting the most from enquiry.

The 'Before You Go' box on the planning grid is your opportunity to explore all the prior learning needed for certain projects or topics. It is also the chance for you to identify the gaps in enquiry experience and skills needed to make projects successful.

For example, exploring electricity means that children should have experience of what objects at home or school use electricity and require safety around electricity.

Similarly, in maths, before children can do addition, they need to know numbers and labelling of groups of numbers, as well as knowing what 'more' and 'less' mean.

So now you've done some of the groundwork to prepare yourself and your school for an enquiry journey. Try to do all the preparation in 'Before You Go' so that you feel confident in presenting and leading staff meetings to others.

# 3

# Who's going with you?

**Figure 3.1**

> The secret of change is to focus all of your energy, not on fighting the old, but on building the new.
>
> *Aristotle*

There is a group of teachers in your school who are usually more comfortable with taking risks, asking open-ended questions and bringing a sense of humour to the classroom. You'll need this group to help bring about change. They may well feel at ease with a loosening of timetables, organisation and de-cluttering of the curriculum. Use the group of teachers that you've recognised as Team Enquiry and allow them to help you promote the view that enquiry is a positive experience that motivates learners. There will be another group of teachers who are a little more sceptical: still good teachers and very solid in their understanding of teaching and learning, but a little more hesitant to change, or rather they want to see it work before plunging in.

This group are generally good organisers and well established in the school and very productive within the whole life of the school, although maybe their impact needs to be challenged more. At times, this type of teacher brings enquiry to their teaching, though it is usually quite structured and not so flexible. The learning outcomes are quite fixed before starting, so no surprises can occur. This teacher feels less safe in having a go and letting the children decide for themselves, believing that they know best.

*This is your first target!!*

Enquiry opportunities have to be amazing for this group of teachers to begin to change. So your first experience of delivering enquiry training has to work. These teachers are less likely to have a go at an enquiry lesson with little preparation. Therefore, be very clear that planning time is essential before the enquiry approach gets started.

There are teachers who, whilst still being good teachers, will find an enquiry model difficult to adopt. It doesn't instantly attract them and it will take more investment from you and Team Enquiry for them to see the benefits. Always be optimistic that you will reach them and that there will be enquiry elements that they will bring to their practice. In conversations about improving outcomes, they are more likely to say teaching to tests and teaching children how to answer question papers is the best way to improve results. Their window of enquiry experience is narrow and they've not allowed themselves to go with the flow.

They are afraid of being flexible because they see it as a weakness. They are usually quite controlling and stick to a plan and are not willing to go off at a tangent unless they control it. We need to give these teachers room and space to see teachers doing it well and that their role in the whole school initiative is vital. They may not enjoy doing it at first, but they cannot let the children in their care miss out on the enquiry experience. That will just lead to demoralised children.

What a way to get a section going! Sorry – we will talk more about how to empower staff later in Platform 7: 'Letting go'.

Hold on to the positives and in that way, by promoting Team Enquiry and making their enquiry experiences amazing, you will not give anyone an opportunity to see enquiry in a negative light. Make the most of those teachers who are willing to have a go. The more you know about your staff the better – play to their strengths, give them recognition, display positive experiences and make the training fun and creative.

Find out how the staff feel about enquiry. For my school, I devised a questionnaire to help gauge where the school's starting point was (Figure 3.2).

This generated lots of questions about teachers' concerns about enquiry. These were used to find common themes and questions. It also most importantly gave a feeling for the attitude and mood towards enquiry.

Many concerns for my school focussed around the children's ability to access and enjoy enquiry; that enquiries shouldn't be a bolt-on but rather be embedded throughout the curriculum. So, as a result of this, we jointly discussed how to resolve these concerns rather than allowing them to become

# Questionnaire

Name:_____

- How confident are you at understanding different levels of questioning?

| 😃 | 🙂 | 😐 | 😟 | 😣 |
|----|----|----|----|----|
| 5 | 4 | 3 | 2 | 1 |

- If confident ( 4 or 5) please give examples of your understanding.

- If less confident (1 or 2) please give reasons for this.

What do you love about the enquiry days?

Do you have any reservations about enquiry days? What are they?

**Figure 3.2**   Staff questionnaire

barriers. Further staff meetings were then built on from positive experiences so that meetings were held together to give support and sharing of ideas, and 'wow' days would become a celebration of a term's work rather than separate sessions. It was music to my ears to hear that they wanted enquiry to run through the curriculum, be timetabled and not be a stand-alone activity. Brilliant! – now we needed to see that in action, so future staff meetings involved bringing enquiry to the everyday. After doing just a few 'wow' enquiry days the staff could already see its worth and were now ready to embed it into teaching and learning.

This initial questionnaire and first staff meeting would inform future planning times so use the information to organise a discussion pathway for future training and meetings. Note your pathway on the reflection page (Figure 3.3).

This is just an example; yours will have meaning and clarity to your school's enquiry journey (e.g. *questioning → engagement → 'wow' days → engaging parents → enquiry skills → assessment*).

New initiatives can be exciting and inspiring, but they only work if your school needs them and makes them their own. Finding the right place to start is important and because it's a whole-school approach you have to start with everyone so that it has high impact and high outcomes. Starting with just Team Enquiry will go a long way in embedding an enquiry approach. The doubters will only make your attention follow them, so don't let negativity bring enquiry down. They will be difficult to open up to new ideas but go ahead with it anyway. They may be carried along with the enthusiasm of the committed, which will worry them, but keep your focus on the bigger picture. You are doing this to make the children better learners. No one can argue with that and you are more than willing to listen to their constructive ideas. Don't allow yourself to be distracted from the end game – you'll be amazed at how many teachers feel the same – I give you permission not to feel guilty!

The first staff meeting needs to be monumental – I'm not putting pressure on you! Make it fun, personal and engaging. I decided that they needed a boost of creative thinking, so I placed a few interesting objects out on each table – for example a shark tooth fossil, rusty keys and an old ammunition box. This was the foundation work activity before asking them to jump into the deep end of enquiry. Take care to group people – remember your audience and their characters. I played a game first to pair people up with someone they don't usually talk to. The session involved imagining that a child had brought one of these objects into school and that the children would spend some time doing activities based around them. This is quite a 'safe' activity for primary teachers who, generally, are quite good at this sort of thing: non-threatening, creative and collaborative.

**Figure 3.3** Reflection page

**Figure 3.4**

Why don't you have a go? Use the photo in Figure 3.4 as a stimulus and make notes around the edge.

Describe the object.

What is it made of?

How do you know?

What else is made of the same thing?

There was a 'buzz' in the room, just as I'd imagined. Even the quietest members of staff who usually gave very little during discussions started holding, talking, imagining and creating. They actually acknowledged that they had come up with some interesting ideas. One teacher who was unsure at first about what to expect really enjoyed the session and wanted to do it again. They asked if they could bring their own things in next time.

We rarely get time to come together and be creative collaboratively. You may not think you have time, but I can assure you that it will be 20 minutes well spent. The session was a positive experience and stimulated discussions and sharing of ideas where everyone contributed.

Use this time during the discussion to practise your facilitating skills, by going in and listening to ideas and threads of creativity. Bring the whole group together and give praise, and respond to lines of enquiry by asking:

"How can we find that out?"

"What would happen if we put it here?"

By using these higher-order questioning techniques it's a good chance for you to practise and for others to see you do it. At the end of the session ask staff to reflect on the best bits and what improvements could be made. How would they present to children? Get them used to being critical and creative thinkers.

Use this opportunity to think about the verbal and non-verbal messages that you are giving (Figure 3.5). How well did you take on the role of a facilitator?

"What did you do?"

"What did you say?"

This is a good starting point for the children too. Use a circle time or discussion time to talk about certain objects and encourage the children to ask questions about it. If you're in EYFS or Year 1 the children bring in things all the time. Just remember that you need to probe on a deeper level than just description, so that the children are using their questioning skills and their ideas are being valued. Sometimes the best ideas are not delivered or presented in the clearest way, so encourage thinking by being positive in your response. You need to do this activity several times and practise with the children how to ask questions. For example:

"What did you notice?"

"I like your thinking."

"How can we use this outside?"

An environment of talking and explaining needs to be nurtured. Encouraging the children to explain what they are doing and why they are doing it like that is so important in making them self-aware and responsible for their own learning.

During staff meetings and natural discussions in the staff room, you will now have recognised Team Enquiry and you are going to use this team to see the best in enquiry for others. Build on this! Continue to keep enquiry in the

**Figure 3.5** Reflection page

forefront of people's minds and share the enquiry pathway with staff so that it is transparent and purposeful. Team Enquiry will art to grow, but only if you nurture it and continue the development of enquiry as a teaching style to enhance learning, not an 'out with the old, in with the new' mentality.

If you are leading enquiry in school, and in further staff meetings or training sessions, you could use Team Enquiry to filter through this positive view of enquiry. They are like a secret society of forward-thinking people who, without really knowing it, manage to embrace new ideas and the notion of facilitating.

During planning meetings you could mix the staff around so that there is a balance between 'raring to go' teachers and more reserved teachers. In this way, meetings are lively yet supportive. Just as you would match children together for certain activities in the classroom to allow less confident personalities to mingle with leaders, you need to do the same here with the staff. Working collaboratively will help everyone to see enquiry from all sides and approach ideas for new enquiries from a variety of ways.

If you aren't leading enquiry then it's about changing your own practice and reflecting on your own role in meetings and discussions to bring your own 'open-mindedness' to enquiry teaching. Hopefully, your training will have included an enquiry approach as well as being positive to new initiatives. You need time to consolidate your experiences though, just as the children do. The responses I usually get from new teachers is that they've not had enough experience yet or they want to fit in with how the school does things. I appreciate this; you need to remember that adapting your teaching methods and trying new things will make others around you feel positively about you and view you as a teacher who wants to learn and improve.

Be confident in your views and celebrate what you have learnt so far and don't forget you are fresh out of training with the most up-to-date knowledge of curriculum, teaching and learning initiatives. You have a lot to bring to enquiry teaching as well as the positive impetus for other staff. Whatever role you have in the school now is the time to get yourself well established in Team Enquiry. Be honest with yourself and decide that you can be the enquiry teach that is going to embrace the facilitator role.

I often use staff meetings and team meetings not to tell people what we are going to do but to open up to others, generating the discussion or establishing the problematic issues. As a team, we would then try to come up with solutions or ways forward. In doing this you are again being non-confrontational and not appearing as the expert but rather being the gatherer and collator of issues. They've answered their own questions.

This approach needs to flow between staff and children so that everyone is being reflective, flexible and collaborative. You know the strengths and weaknesses of your children and what skills they need to practise in order to become better learners. So, on the planning grid, note down which groups of children need to practise certain skills.

This is also the perfect opportunity to decide which members of staff are responsible for certain areas. For example, that teacher would be perfect for creating a timetable or permission slip or checking the outdoor equipment. In an open and non-judgemental team, some teachers may acknowledge that they need more experience with playing or evaluating, so use this space on the planning grid to delegate roles or skills to be developed.

You should now have a better understanding of the types of teachers around you. If you are an enquiry leader, you'll be able to continue your approach towards the different personalities around you and tailor discussions or training sessions to support the skills set out there. You will definitely have recognised who is on Team Enquiry and who is nearly there; remember those are your priorities as a leader and if you're a new teacher then they are the teachers you need to align yourself with. They are the ones who are going to be most receptive to a new way of teaching and you need to make your alliances with them. You could end up working with them more closely in the future, so strengthen that bond now.

# 4

# The Itinerary

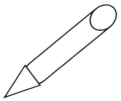

**Figure 4.1**

Because the planning in some schools is quite defined, you should become familiar with how Early Years teams plan staff discussions and 'pooling' of ideas. It not only shares ideas, it also causes the team to bond. Being respectful of ideas and valuing them is part of team building, thereby creating an environment where ownership and responsibility will be reflected in the children's learning behaviours.

Among the different ways enquiry can be facilitated in the classroom, planning and preparation are the constants. This will give support to less confident or inexperienced teachers and will also give an invisible structure to the day, topic or sequence of lessons for everyone.

Ask for staff meeting time so that teams can plan for enquiry and have it as their priority. Issues around coverage will always lurk around these discussions, so have curriculum objectives and long-term planning available. Don't let coverage highjack the meeting, as all teachers have the pressure of making sure they've covered the correct unit or given appropriate weighting to certain objectives.

This time should be used to focus on the enquiry skills and how they fit into the curriculum, as well as the child's experience in the classroom.

Building on prior learning and experiences is always a good place to start planning for the future. If children can make links to previous learning, then they are going to approach an enquiry lesson positively. If it's the first time then you have to pitch your planning and organisation appropriately. Also, if it's the first time for staff you need to visit the 'All aboard!' and 'Before you go' sections for this to have real purpose. Let's assume you have done these and there is a climate of openness to enquiry. Spend more time on these areas if not. It's taken me several years to be anywhere near making enquiry embedded in the daily practice.

Teachers feel very safe planning with the people on their team; teachers who they have been working with for a long time, so take this opportunity to mix some teams up. Maybe swap Heads of Years around and introduce a whole-school theme that then every team can start from. Use the School Development Plan (SDP) to find gaps in skills or threads that are being tackled throughout the school, for example questioning, inference, and creativity. Use these as starting points.

The Itinerary is the basic structure of the day once you have the principles in place. Remember, if anyone says "I don't enjoy enquiry because it lacks structure; it's too open", this is the part where you devise the timetable. Bear in mind that the Destination (Platform 4) should support the itinerary as you really need to know what you want the children to get from the session. I've put this section before to try and settle the nerves of those who need a plan and feel more confident with an itinerary. You must do this section with teams so that everyone is on board and ideas and information are communicated. You may end up creating a separate timetable with questions, times, groups and places clearly labelled. Figure 4.2 shows an example to give you an idea.

Really focus on what everyone will be doing on the day, the process of learning and questioning rather than the product. Whilst planning, try to link everything together so that the questions will be explored through the enquiry. I suppose enquiry is associated with knowledge and understanding the world or science topics. It can also be applied to any curriculum subject. For example, one of my school's enquiry days was to do with art, music and performing arts. You might be thinking … why? But it grabbed attention and enthused staff and that enthusiasm would, hopefully, transfer to the children. We also did it at the end of the half-term as a celebration of all we had learnt so far. There's nothing like a bit of dressing up to motivate and excite, so we based the day around musicals and artists.

It might be that you rotate groups of children around investigations, or use questions gathered from prior learning activities to be explored – this will create a sequence of investigations. Some may directly explore a question and some may help children to practise the skills of enquiry.

Bearing this in mind, the structure of the day or session should allow the learners to use their skills. Some of the activities need to have little teacher presence in order to let **creativity** flow. Someone always watching them can hinder the development of creative skills.

| | |
|---|---|
| Water Exploration<br><br>Foil water slides on the hill<br><br>Guttering coming from water trays<br><br>Foil boats for sticks with bowls of water | Dens<br><br>Walk to the woods with 'mini - me' milk bottles.<br><br><br>Making dens for our 'mini - me' bottles. |
| Magic Walk<br><br>Taking empty milk bottles on our walk around school grounds. Add little things to your bottle as we go and choose a favourite stick to take back with you.<br><br>Winding wool wand station, potion jugs & lids.<br><br>Potion lists & cauldron | 'Stick at it' challenges!<br><br>Ordering a selection of sticks according to size<br><br><br>Stick initials (capital letters)<br><br><br>Biggest stick challenge. How many lolly sticks long is your stick? Recording totals |

Outdoor

Classroom

Day!

| | |
|---|---|
| 9am | Register & gather on EYFS hill for story |
| 9.30–10.15am | **GROUP ACTIVITY 1** |
| 10.15–10.45am | Outdoor snacks, milk and SINGING |
| 10.45–1130am | **GROUP ACTIVITY 2** |
| 11.30–11.45am | Inside for photo reviews & hand washing etc. |
| LUNCH | LUNCH |
| 1.00–1.15am | Register & Storytime |
| 1.15–2.00pm | **GROUP ACTIVITY 3** |
| 2.00–2.45pm | **GROUP ACTIVITY 4** |
| 2.45–3.15pm | Classroom for clean-up, songs, photo reviews etc. |
| 3.15pm | HOMETIME! |

**Figure 4.2**   Example of timetable

You may need time to talk about this with teams. Discuss what they think hinders their own creativity and what stops the *thinking, learning* and *creative* flow in children. You could even do a pupil voice with your own class to find out what stops them from being creative, such as over-confidence and the unwillingness to try something new. Try asking the following question: what are you not very good at but like doing? (See Figure 4.3).

It might be that you want to develop the creative, thinking or *questioning* skills of your children, so allow time for these to be explained; this should be a whole-school focus. If you want your school to be an enquiry school then everyone should be on board with stopping teaching to tests and promoting individual's *motivation to enquire* and a *'can do' attitude* as well as *welcoming a challenge*, with an emphasis on *reflecting* on next steps.

The activities throughout the day should have a balance between developing all these skills. Underpinning all of this is communication, leading learning and curriculum skills. For example; creative writing about a safari requires talking to each other about your senses of what you can see, hear, feel or know is there. Organising each other as to who is going to find out or lead the discussion and then the literacy ability to write down your ideas. Ample time needs to be given from an early age for these skills to be allowed to bloom. Younger children will be amazing at the talking creatively stages but may not be so confident with the writing skills, and as they become older it can flip over. Why not allow all age groups to mingle so that they can learn from each other and older children have the chance to take part in creative discussions?

For example, during the same safari enquiry, Year 6 children buddied up with Reception and discussed a safari photograph. The Year 6s had the opportunity to lead the literacy element through writing, something the whole school was developing through the School Development Plan. Reception had the valuable experience of seeing writing being modelled. whilst both sets of children shared ideas, thoughts and reflections – in this way learning and communications skills flourish and deepen. One class may need an audience for a presentation from their peers, so explore these ideas.

Mixed in with all this activity should also be a fair balance of curriculum objectives. As we've mentioned before some, teachers get worried that the coverage isn't there in enquiry sessions. So, make sure you are making links to the curriculum; this is where the best learning takes place: in finding links with geography, literacy, art and PE. Again, the safari theme was amazing for this as the children can explore so many skills and objectives in one hit.

For example, describing a safari scene requires geographical knowledge of where it is and what is there. A useful strategy for provoking questioning and thinking is to put an 'odd one out' or 'red-herring' into the situation. This can

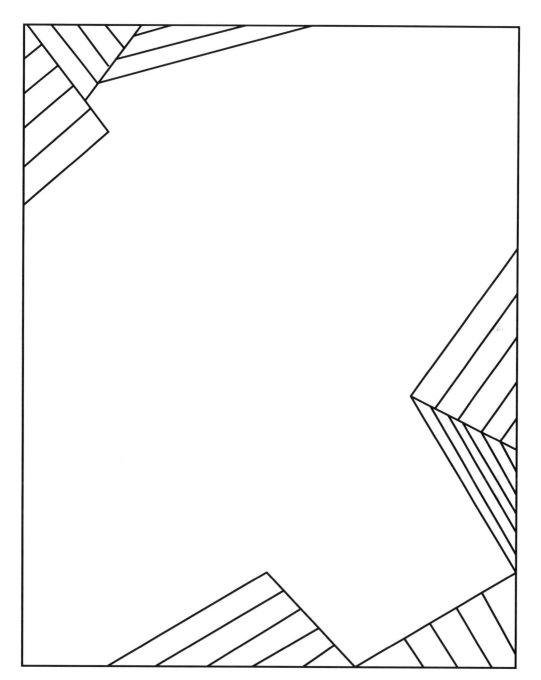

**Figure 4.3** Reflection page

stir up some interesting questions and thought processes. It allows the discussion for why that shouldn't be there. It challenges misconceptions, which then allows deeper learning to take place. We had a wide range of animals to be placed in our small world safari. There was a lot of chatting going on about why there was a tiger and a panda there, but if we had only put safari animals on offer, then a whole lot of understanding would have been missed with children making decisions within a restricted context given to them on a platter.

Talking about why those animals shouldn't be there was invaluable. It allowed some individuals to argue the case that they don't belong there and others to hear that knowledge and then apply it to their own play, a few days later this was retained. It would be interesting to know when a similar scenario is revisited next term whether they can still apply this knowledge or question which object is the 'odd one out'. If you do this regularly enough throughout the school, it makes learners always ready and alert to their understanding being challenged. Use the reflection page (Figure 4.4) to develop possible odd one out or red herring provocations.

There are also literacy skills to communicate ideas as well as artistic reflection about colours, textures and mood of photographs. We did a yoga/dance session where we explored animal movements and poses. The children could then create their own animal dance sequence.

Use the enquiry theme to capture the many different objectives and skills – make those links obvious to all.

The adults' role is crucial in all this. You may have confident staff around you who can lead these activities, or you may be on your own. Make bonds with other staff as best you can, so that you aren't doing everything!

Refer back to Platform 3 – who's going with you? Be clear about roles and responsibilities with all the adults. If you are on your own then the balance of independent, practising or creative activities will be greater than if you have a team. Just be very clear with the team about who's doing what, where and when. I've done it in a few different ways and what I've learnt that works best is keeping the same group of children and rotating them around the activities during the day or session. It gives you time to deepen the discussions with those children; plus each activity is new to you too, so that you can learn alongside the children. What a great learning role model you are!

You may want to stay with the activity and just rotate the children. However, I've found that the repetition does not give me joy – I remember doing a circus theme day and my activity was juggling. By the end of the day I looked like a very sad and dejected clown.

As much as you can, use the outside environment to enhance your enquiries. It's not just an extra space you can utilise, but also a valuable resource for gathering, noticing patterns and exploring change. Going outside can

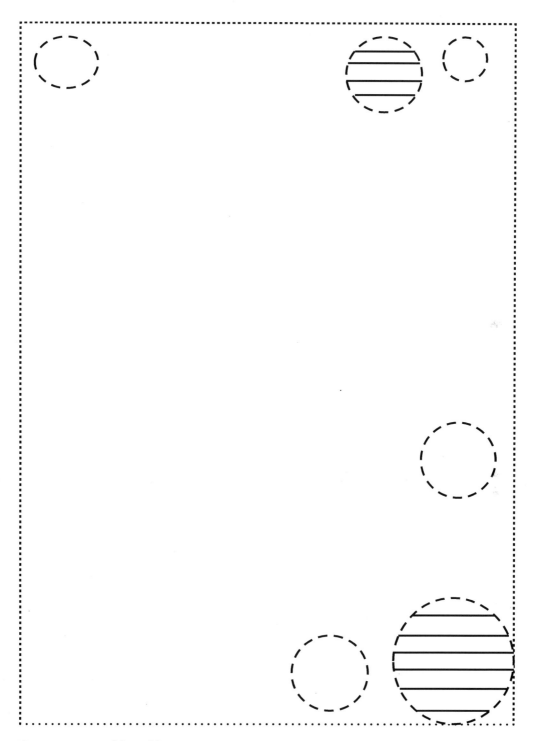

**Figure 4.4**  Possible red herrings

become a great adventure for going on seasonal walks, but use it every day as an extension to your classroom.

On some occasions, the school has taken part in national schemes to encourage children to spend all day outside and link it to science investigations, or work done by charities. However you use it, make sure you incorporate it into your practice. You can easily make those links again across the curriculum, incorporating physical activity with number hunts, animal habitats or growing plants. Getting involved in a practical way will strengthen the reason why we're doing something. Six months after moving compost and digging planters, the children still remembered that event and were able to respond when I asked them why we were doing it.

It had relevance as well as their remembering the conditions needed for plants to grow. The children could appreciate why we were doing it, but it was their hard work that had got the plants to grow and not labelling a diagram of the parts of a plant, or listing things that a plant needs to grow.

At the same time, you can promote physical activity and a healthy lifestyle, along with enquiry skills and the curriculum.

Teachers in Early Years will see the classroom and outside area as an extra teacher. It's about trying to incorporate that view further up the school, in order for older children to regularly access the outdoor environment more frequently than during PE lessons.

This stage would also be a good time to plan for speakers or specialists to visit schools. Local artists, high school teachers or specialist teachers will strengthen community links. It can be expensive too, so use the links you have with local shops, parents and ex-pupils to bring questioning alive.

For example, we brought in a mystery speaker during a family history enquiry. The children had photographs of the speaker from different stages of her life and a few objects like toys. The children asked questions to establish who this person was, their age, etc. It was brilliant to watch some children making links to their own experiences. They found out that the speaker was a grandma, so we had lots of discussion about that. The children were able to make links between all the evidence given to them, to be a detective and to work out whom this person was without actively being told. They had to infer all the clues to fill in the gaps in the speaker's identity. The speaker was actually my mum! What an interesting way of getting children talking about family history, toys from the past and questioning that helps to fit information together to create meaning.

Finance always crops up when teachers are planning – there is often not the money to buy equipment or go on trips, or to get specialist speakers in. So use what resources you have wisely. Find ways of being resourceful with

**Figure 4.5**

any funding that you have. Often the most memorable enquiries cost little money. When I did the questionnaire with teachers about their enquiry reservations, resources and finance was a concern, but this should not be a barrier or an excuse to not do it. Ask the children to bring things in to school or take photographs of places they've been to, to then support an enquiry. As a team, work around this issue and discuss it to seek a solution that works best for your school.

If you are going to invest in resources, let them be high quality, durable and versatile, so that they can be used for a variety of purposes.

Where appropriate, use the real thing, obviously not if it's breakable, but our children deserve beautiful resources displayed in an attractive way. This not only enhances play but also develops skills in looking after property and valuing belongings, as well as exploring different textures and properties. Children need to have experience of playing and handling real objects like a ceramic cup so they can learn to use it and move it safely (Figure 4.5).

# 5

# Destination

**Figure 5.1**

As mentioned earlier, Destination goes hand-in-hand with Itinerary and both need to be considered when planning enquiries and developing an enquiry school. Subject leaders should know what the priorities are for the school and these can run through the enquiries like a thread. There should be a focus on the skills needed to enhance the curriculum and enquiries. For example, writing is often a priority for schools, so ensure that writing opportunities are provided to support enquiries. This can be done effectively by ensuring there is a recording or writing element to the session, whether it's adults or older children modelling writing to others, or children recording results or describing scenes. Make those cross-curricular links and in doing so you will gather evidence for subject leaders which will be valuable in their attempts to show how their subject is impacting the whole school. You will have to gather this evidence for them or organise the channels to share this information.

To establish common destinations, try doing an audit of workbooks and lessons. This will give you a measure of how enquiry is feeding into the curriculum and at what level. You can then check consistency between classes and progression between year groups, which can further inform future destinations. It might be that consistency between classes needs to be a focus to ensure that children are getting the same enquiry diet.

If you aren't an enquiry leader, you may feel that this is not something you can suggest. However, between classes in your year groups it would be a very useful exercise. Wanting there to be consistency between year groups and making sure you are providing the same as other classes is a commendable trait, so give it a go. Learning mentors should already be making sure that this is happening so that you're all being proactive in strengthening consistency.

There must be clarity regarding your destination in order for all the hard work you have put in during 'All aboard!' and 'Before you go' now needs to pay dividends. It's not going to happen all of a sudden, but everyone needs to be on board and able to see the links between enquiry, skills, subjects and school development.

During a staff meeting, gather all the subject priority statements and ask the staff to see if there is common ground. This is a good exercise to see if the priorities have enough direction and also if there are common themes. By doing this you are tying together the numerous priorities for the school but also tapping into the talent of the staff for galvanising the school development plan into action. Once enquiry can be seen as all-encompassing – reaching through subjects, learning, teaching and ethos – then its value will be unquestionable. Use the reflection page to note down school priorities and ideas around the school motto or vision statement. If you haven't got one ... create one! (See Figure 5.2.)

Whether it's a questioning or inference priority, problem solving or reflection enquiry, all lend themselves to enquiry; therefore, it must become top of the agenda for all subject leaders. And you can't really say you've had an impact until the identified priorities are being visited on a daily basis, that there is evidence of it and changes to performance happen. Pulling those threads of priority together can only benefit the way children learn and teachers provide for learning. Teaching subjects in isolation is only going to make children compartmentalise; as a result, when presented with activities where they have to apply to new situations, they could struggle. Whereas if they are confident in switching from one strategy or skill to another, then their problem-solving skills should become a lot more successful.

You need to plan in regular update meetings for enquiry to make sure the momentum is building and that everyone can reflect on the impact it is having.

Some destinations may be different for different phases and this is fine and appropriate, but there's nothing like a whole-school focus to really bring it all together and it's also much clearer for everyone to jump on-board with.

Once your priorities are established then so are your destinations. It's not just the end product, remember, it's the process and skill opportunities that are provided. On one level it could be a meal that has been created but, more crucially, it's the devising of a menu, buying the ingredients, reading

**Figure 5.2**  Priority reflection page

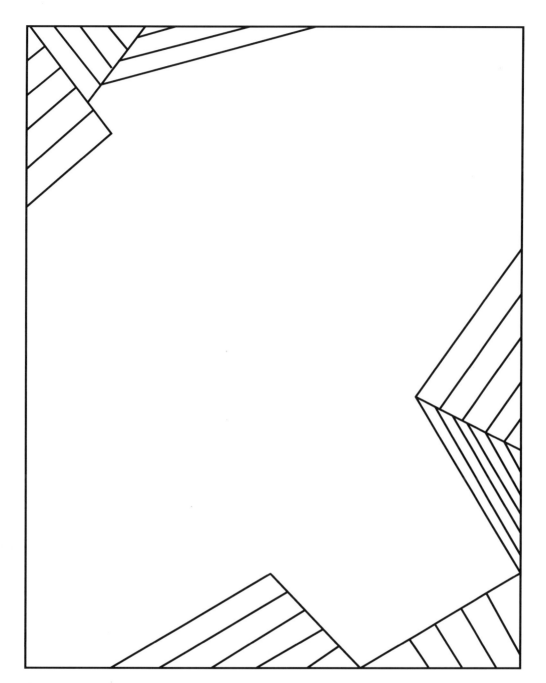

**Figure 5.3** Reflection page

the recipe and following instructions. These skills are the real destination, and just think of the cross-curricular links that are needed to do this activity. Furthermore, subject leaders should want to know that this is going on.

Keep going with the sharing process; if you stop and leave it as a 'one-off' activity then it will be forgotten. Keep those destinations in everyone's mind and join forces with other schools that are at a similar stage. You will need to plan out which priorities are being explored and involve the relevant subject leaders for maximum impact.

Always bear in mind that if the children are aware of this process that the staff are going through, then they are clear about the future of their learning from speaking to children right through the school. In my school, the message was that they were aware of their own and other classes' approaches to enquiry and they wanted a slice of the enquiry cake. If they saw one class doing it then why weren't they? So, if as a whole school you can adopt the same or similar destinations that are appropriate for your children then it would be fair, relevant and meaningful. Therefore, link your destinations to common values, the school motto or SDP to make the experience purposeful for everyone. Be clear about your destinations on your planning grid. Too many will make it difficult to follow and confusing. Pick out the priorities discussed earlier that will make enquiry successful and share them with all enquirers.

The destinations need to be a tangible goal with the whole school followed in keeping on board. Use the reflection page to develop possible destinations (Figure 5.3).

# 6

# Check-in

**Figure 6.1**

This is a good way to start an enquiry and it doesn't have to be on the same subject as the enquiry. It's a vehicle for children to start thinking and talking. It's a bit like a warm-up before you start playing the sport or like a sketch before the painting or even a canapé before the main course.

It needs to be linked to feelings and emotions for the children to emotionally invest in the question or idea. Usually, the best way to deliver this is through a circle time. The check-in is like the warm-up idea for you to think about. For example, what is your favourite place to visit and why? Also it's a time to establish the ground rules for enquiry so that discussions about respecting ideas, taking turns and being mindful of each other are very important in order for the deeper questioning to occur. There are no right or wrong answers to this. It's about opening up and justifying an opinion.

One of my favourites is to ask, can you tell me something that is green? I love listening to the different and varied answers. I have an understanding with one child who often says something unusual and I often use his observations to inspire other children. Maybe you have a child like this? It raises the expectation for others so that other children think more creatively. When asked to think of something red, we had ladybird, felt-tip and strawberries. This child said 'scotch bonnet'! This was very intriguing and we had a whole explanation of how, when and where they had come to know about it.

On a different occasion the question was, can you think of something in the sky? Many children replied bird and aeroplane but the air of expectation had been raised by the first child, so we also had clouds, pollen and one child said, "Nana, she was my friend but she's in heaven now." This came from a very quiet and timid child who had struggled with settling into school and had lots of issues around transition. It was amazing to hear such a profound and heartfelt answer from a child who had not given much up to this point. I would never have known their thoughts if that 'big picture' question had not been asked and the high expectation of meaningful and interesting answers not been set.

For this to really work well with children, it needs to be done frequently so that the rules of circle time are habitual. It may very well lead onto a topic that you want to further investigate. For example, what is art? Use this as a check-in question before exploring the artwork of a famous artist. Or, what does 'wild' mean as in a 'wild animal'? This could then lead on to the role of animal charities or zoos.

Circle time check-ins make a clear start to enquiry sessions that can be your chance to ask those big questions that make children wonder about things and instils curiosity. The enquiry champion Kath Murdoch promotes lots of practical and interesting ideas about enquiry in general, although I particularly enjoy listening to her thoughts on big questions and implementing enquiry into the every day.

Starting off an enquiry in this way very quickly gives you a gauge of who may need support for this session. If someone is very quiet and reticent then that will help you and other children to support and encourage where necessary. Also if someone is dominant and opinionated, a check-in gives you the opportunity to channel this enthusiasm and again refocus the group on being respectful and valuing others' ideas. Once children and staff become familiar with elements of enquiry, they will become confident enough to participate. The staff need to be part of the circle too, so make sure there is enough room and space for everyone to feel comfortable. You can be a positive role model and participate alongside the class, making them view you as a fellow learner.

Children need to see you learning and thinking with them, making spontaneity a strength to be celebrated rather than a weakness to be avoided. Going on a journey together is powerful and adapting and clarifying as you go along demonstrates a resilient learner. That's the kind of role model I want to be.

Many teachers have concerns that enquiry sessions are too flexible for some children who do not enjoy a less structured day. However, I think that the check-in activity can establish the rules and organisation of the session and gives everyone the platform to share worries and concerns from the start. Armed with this knowledge you can adjust accordingly. Look for and promote those characteristics of learning which will empower your children to do the best that they are capable of. I'm sure you will be surprised at how conscientious and heartfelt answers and ideas can be once the opportunity is given.

**Figure 6.2** Reflection page

Having the opportunity to explain why they feel this way and justify their thoughts will help them incredibly later when they may be asked questions and they need to communicate to a group about their ideas. The check-in is a practice run for clarifying their own beliefs and thoughts and articulating their ideas confidently, knowing that there is a captive audience willing them on and supporting them.

Listening is a major part of this too, so be a positive role model in listening to ideas and thoughts. Watch your body language and eye contact as this also promotes the idea of valuing others. Play games where listening is vital to the purpose of the game. Listening and hearing the ideas of others will consolidate their own thoughts and allow them to appreciate that we all have different viewpoints.

Once you've tried out the check-in activity you have set the scene for further discussion for opening the enquiry. This is the right time to share the organisation of the day or session as well as set the ground rules of expectations to make it successful and memorable.

Discuss with your team what possible check-in questions you could have – remember to think big! (See Figure 6.2.)

# Letting go

**Figure 7.1**

A colleague once said that they used to think that it was how much experience a teacher had that meant they could 'wing it'. However, after developing enquiry during staff meetings, they came to see it as a skill rather than experience. This goes to show that if change is imposed it is impossible to have an impact, so instead we have to see and witness for ourselves the facilitator style bringing confidence.

In this platform, you will be encouraged to empower teachers to see that 'winging it' is not a weakness but rather a skill which needs fostering and nurturing just like any other skill.

It's almost like you need a toolkit of strategies to enable you to practise 'winging it' (see Figure 7.2).

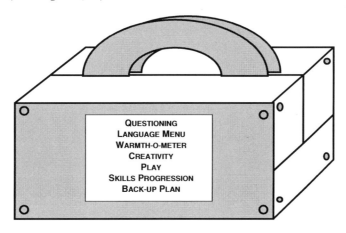

**Figure 7.2**

So what should go in the toolkit?

Let's look at these skills more closely.

## Questioning

You need to know the different levels of questioning and to share this regularly with your staff. It's easy to do this once as part of a 'wow' day, but regular practice will embed this into the whole-school approach. It's integral to your school's unique selling point that we teach enquiry by following all the 'toolkit' elements to different levels of questioning being the key to an opening.

Questioning should focus on the less obvious – more on the imagination and creativity of your learners. Open-ended questions are going to create a multitude of answers which can be explored, so making this a permanent feature in your teaching is vital. We need to help our children think about things in a variety of ways and we are the role models in this. Just like in English lessons we promote what a good piece of writing looks like, we need to make our questioning clear and purposeful. Reception children are ready to understand what a question mark is and the starter words that turn statements into questions: who, what, when, where and how.

Always include questions about approaches – for example:

"How would you do this?"

"Have you done something similar before?"

These are important to connect prior learning and application to new situations. Give opportunities for questions that stimulate self-monitoring – such as:

"How do you know you're right?"

"What might help you?"

This helps children to think in chunks and see progress as you're going along rather than in a blitz at the end when it's too late to change. An evaluation at the end of an activity was always seen as good practice and it's easy to organise as a teacher – but in a plenary session at the end of a topic or activity it is quite straightjacketing. In life, we tweak as we go along. If you're putting up a shelf, you don't wait until the end to decide it's wonky – you amend as you go along.

Using questions to make connections between similar activities is also a strategy that needs to go in the 'toolkit'. Questions about how children approached a certain task last time help to firm up self-monitoring and pattern-seeking enquiries.

"How did you do this before?"

"Could it help you now?"

Are the children making links – encourage them by being that good role model again.

"Did anyone notice how we did this last time? "

"Could that way help us this time?"

Making questioning and thinking out loud go hand in hand, which will give the children a rich and varied vocabulary around how we think – that has to go in the toolkit! This will ultimately give them and you confidence to enquire. Be very explicit in your choice of questions so that it becomes a thread throughout the whole session, with questions and thinking bouncing around the room as a ripple that keeps going, rather than a yes/no answer, which often leads to silence! For example:

"What do you think about that?"

"Why did that happen?"

In Early Years, questioning happens spontaneously during an activity or play. Sometimes you may have a set objective with an appropriate activity as a vehicle, such as using cubes to measure the length of an object. Or a child might be pretending to be a giant and be making large footsteps because they have just heard the story of *Jack and the Bean Stalk*. Instead of pulling them to you to do the activity, you go to them and join in with giant stepping. This is when questioning can go to further depths because the child is already hooked in; therefore it is child led.

More importantly, you can ask those questions that encourage children to reason:

"I wonder how many giant steps will fill along the gate?"

"I wonder if your giant step is longer than mine?"

"Can you estimate how many steps long I am?"

Taking this questioning further still, you could then ask the child to sequence the objects they've measured in order from shortest to longest. They may even measure their giant step with a metre ruler and notice the scale along the edge in centimetres.

"What are these?"

"What are they for?"

This is using the questioning tool to really encourage children to think and reason. Another good example in maths in Early Years and also into Key Stage 1 is to have blank grids available for children to create their own counting games. I've seen examples of a beanstalk game board with spaces on the leaves for children to either jump counters along the spaces or write the numbers in from start to finish. I asked one child, "How could you make this trickier?" She decided to write in numbers, counting in twos. This was so informative for me and it was all her idea. So, child led again.

As she filled in the numbers she noticed certain patterns ... "It's all the even numbers." "It's counting in twos so it's one and one more." I asked her then to explain this game to a friend, so she then became the expert of her game and gained satisfaction from watching others enjoy it too. This would work well into Years 1 and 2 when child-initiated games could become more complex and challenging.

This attitude towards questioning can be applied throughout the curriculum. An example of this in story writing happened when a child wanted to write a story but wasn't sure what to write about. So, we played a drawing game where on separate pieces of paper we each drew a face of a person or animal, then folded it over and swapped. Then we drew the arms and body and so on until a figure was complete. This is such an old game but brilliant for bringing humour and problem solving to a story. The figure ended up being a princess with long spaghetti arms. The child then used this prompt to write about how the princess had eaten an apple that had made her arms long so she went to a fairy cottage and asked the fairies to shrink them.

This was not a spoken question I'd posed to the child but a visual drawing that stimulated creative writing to solve the princess's problem. Having prompts for children to respond to and questions to deepen their thinking needs to become commonplace in your classroom. I don't really like lots of text around, making the classroom look too busy and over-stimulating. I prefer pertinent questions and prompts to trigger further learning.

Use Figure 7.3 on the next page to write your favourite questions. Make a list of ones you are definitely going to use in your teaching.

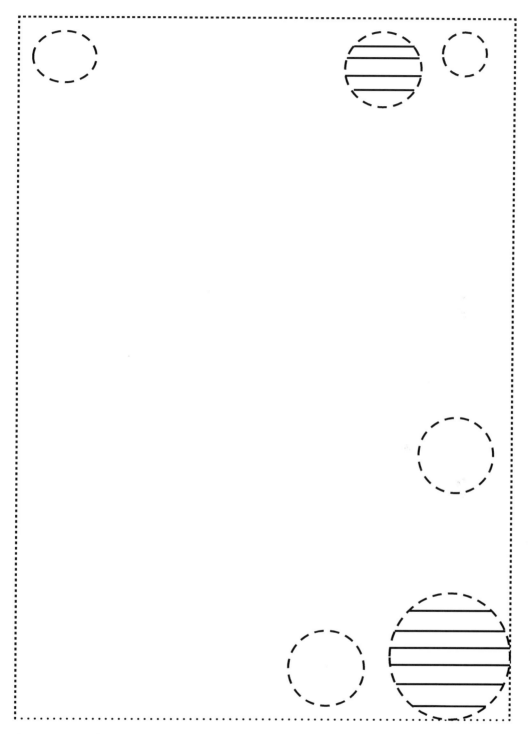

**Figure 7.3** Reflection page

Looking at the bigger picture, thinking and using imagination fits perfectly with an enquiry approach. To start with, enquiry lessons usually take the form of 'wow' or enrichment days. This is a good start for primary schools. Once these days are a regular fixture on the school calendar, you can start to show links to history or science lessons throughout.

## Language menu

Pitching the level and range of vocabulary and language to an enquiry learner is very important. Once you have the prior learning in place, use this to inform the words you choose to promote enquiry. It might be on one level that you want a certain scientific word to be used and understood within the enquiry and/or to promote positive language around learning – for example, resilience, research and evaluate. Be clear from the start – have these words displayed, for example on key rings and flipcharts, and make this part of your enquiry vocabulary.

Often you can refer to these if things are going off on a tangent in order to bring the learning back into line. For example, young children watching ice melt can be very excited and they can get caught up in the hilarity of feeling the ice slip through their fingers, or become fixated with smashing the ice when you want to discuss the properties of ice. Having the key language on the tip of your tongue can steer that conversation back to 'melting' or 'temperature' and even 'focus' and 'concentration'.

Don't be afraid to use this language even with young children in order to get a deeper level of understanding, rather than a superficial level of attacking the ice! I think this is why teachers are worried about these types of sessions, because it's easy to think this is not a valuable activity, whereas what we should be thinking is sitting at a table with a worksheet is *definitely not* a valuable activity. We should be investing our time into building a wide vocabulary and using 'thinking' language within an exciting stimulus and engaging with natural curiosity.

As children move through the primary phase they can become more in control of the language menu necessary to explain a procedure or discuss a narrative. Collaboratively, they should be able to create a list of words that would be useful to write a report or label a diagram. Teachers would need to ensure their words are on the list too, but what a great way to explore technical vocabulary, develop glossaries and make notes.

Whenever I start a new topic in whatever subject, I also start with the knowledge and understanding of vocabulary. I sometimes use it at the check-in stage to explain certain words or to get the children to think of equivalent words. I play the milkshake game where we all think of a delicious milkshake, give it an imaginary shake, drink it and then say mmm. I then ask the children to generate words like yummy, tasty or sweet. I then do the opposite and ask for a disgusting milkshake. To make it even funnier I pretend to be really looking forward to drinking the cobweb, mud and snails milkshake until it reaches my mouth and ... yuck!

Asking for disgusting words is quite entertaining! Give it a try. This game could easily be adapted to other scenarios, for example, "What should I build my house with?" Within this scenario, you could generate a language menu around bricks, scaffolding, cement, etc. Then for the 'silly' materials, such as jelly, the list would be not sturdy, wobbly, unsafe, no foundations.

It's important to recognise that you may not be the only adult facilitating the enquiries, so ensure that all staff and children are aware of the language menus around the class and school. Some teaching assistants will naturally have the skill to help children explore language and develop their vocabulary through open-ended activities. Others may find it less straightforward, so be aware of 'Who is going with you?' on your enquiry journey. Have prompt cards available and vocabulary mats, dictionaries and glossaries to keep them armed for all eventualities.

All children become very proud after learning new words and the definitions. If they learn to use them appropriately and with flair then their confidence will soar and their language menu will become rich and interesting. The only danger is that they use them all at once in their writing with several commas. Over-writing in stories can be difficult to change, so make sure you are modelling the usage of the language menu so that the usage is pertinent. Less is more sometimes!

## Warmth-o-meter

You or a colleague might be feeling decidedly frosty towards the impending enquiry! So here is where the actor's face comes on and you demonstrate your human side. So what if the computer has just crashed! So what if the rain has washed your resources away! Children need to see you being resilient and human. It will only be a disaster if you let it be and we all need to see that calm, caring reaction rather than hysterical, stressful panic because, yet again, my pen has run out.

It's about sharing that human side and being honest about how we react to stressful situations. If we only ever react by being stressed then the outcome will be stressful. We have to exercise our warmth-o-meter and, by showing our calm and caring reaction, defuse the problem and see it not as a weakness, but rather an opportunity to display our warmth and personality. The only way to practise this is to provide opportunities to do it. We probably worry about worst-case scenarios and this is allowed to take over.

As far as I know, no one has been seriously hurt by following an enquiry, so the best strategy is to get out there and do it, and do it with humour and warmth. You can't stop things from going wrong but you can change your reaction to them and that is so valuable in demonstrating to children how to be resilient. If you avoid being outside your comfort zone or, always make everything uber prepared, then you are never really going to know what it feels like to 'wing it' so and will never really make those spontaneous connections with other people. Take the opportunity to make mistakes and get the children to 'mark' your work. You would hope that they wouldn't be scathing because you have been a positive role model and brought warmth to your reaction, and focussed not on the mistake but rather on the next steps to improve.

Recently I went into the hall ready for our first Reception gymnastics lesson. We were all so excited! Brand new PE kits in perfect pump bags. It's a miracle we actually got into the hall with fiddly buttons, shorts over trousers and the usual hilarity when 26 children are all getting changed at once, only to be met with a hall full of other children already in the middle of their gym lesson. There were several reactions I could have taken, from screaming "It's our slot … get out!" to crying uncontrollably at the thought of all the children getting changed back into their uniforms. You'll be pleased to know I chose to exercise my warmth-o-meter on this occasion; I remained like a swan on the exterior and said, "Never mind children, let's go outside." The children never knew my disappointment and, although we did have a hall slot at that time, I chose not to have an argument or crumble but instead to practise my warmth-o-meter.

Another example is when a colleague set up an animal small world with soil, leaves and sticks, a really interesting play activity. However, her reaction when the materials became mixed up and 'messy' was not an example of her using her warmth-o-meter. I suppose working in Early Years has got me used to young children doing this and I have learnt that instead of shouting or blaming them a solution needs to be found. If this is the sort of thing that happens in your class then instead over-reacting badly, be proactive and think about what you need to provide for this behaviour to not interrupt the learning.

Do children need expectations before play? Do these need to be revisited regularly? Do they just need more experience of this sort of small world play so that they become accustomed to expectations? This example was taken from a class in Key Stage 1. The children may have forgotten the high expectations needed to value, care for and play with our resources. They are not to blame for this. They shouldn't be told off for doing this; rather, teachers and teaching assistants need to practise their warmth-o-meter and prepare the children for these scenarios regularly and discuss why it happened and what we need to do to prevent it happening again.

Young children love to collect things, especially early on in the year. Often we would find stones, coins, cubes, dice ... the list goes on! All stuffed into pockets or book boxes or secret corners. This collecting behaviour is natural. Instead of being grumpy and annoyed, provide areas where this behaviour can be celebrated. Tinkering with loose parts can be really satisfying as well as lining objects up or building piles. I remember two children emptying the recycling boxes full of resources for junk modelling and taking them outside to build a dump. The discussion and language from this were remarkable. They talked about plastic, bin lorries and recycling, and at the end, after I had furiously written down my observations, they calmly said, "Right, let's put it back where it belongs." And they did!

A potentially stressful 'untidy' activity became amazing, interesting and knowledgeable because staff had previously exercised their warmth-o-meters and facilitated learning opportunities rather than getting annoyed when things took an unexpected turn that they hadn't planned for.

Being calm and relaxed in classrooms is something we don't always feel. Does it happen enough? In my experience, it can't really happen if you're not doing enquiry teaching. Following a model of everybody doing something at the same time, listening to one speaker and responding in whatever way the speaker wants does not lend itself to enquiry. Rather it is going to generate passive, solitary children with the possibility of conflict and behaviour issues.

If children are engaged, engrossed even, and talking to each other and collaborating then you are setting up an environment for deep-rooted learning to take place. This approach should not just stop at the end of Key Stage 1. Using drama, humour and grouping children will bring out the warmth-o-meter in everyone. Without being sickly and un-genuine; role play, small group work and drama techniques based around real-life experiences can flourish into Key Stage 2. I've seen it happen by using small groups of children to report on different areas of a topic, create a script and then produce a full documentary, which was filmed and then critiqued.

It is possible to bring these techniques into all classes throughout the primary phase and it's even more powerful with older children as it's not boring or static. They are up, moving, talking, performing and evaluating on a constant cycle. This kind of activity is far more memorable and that is the strength of using your enquiry toolkit to facilitate learning as opposed to didactic teaching.

The teaching points from these types of sessions will be clear, pertinent and to the point and children will have the opportunity to explore and wonder as well as actively listen. If you regularly use your warmth-o-meter then responding positively to ideas and scenarios will become second nature. Using your warmth-o-meter means letting go of your limits of how an activity will progress and being fine with that. Once you've had a go I'm sure you'll prefer it and you'll become relaxed in your approach.

Just remember that enquiry is something you do, not who you are. You need to practise the 'winging it' skills in order to be confident. Here, you're trying to create an environment where taking risks is okay. Use the reflection page (Figure 7.4) to confirm how you are going to be warm. What body language and words you are going to use to be empathetic.

## Creativity

You have already by now provided opportunities to be creative with staff. Make this a regular feature of staff meetings. It is okay if your enquiries are art and design based, but if not try to include as much creativity of expression as possible. Do joint planning meetings so that you have a wider audience of thinkers. Recognise the creative potential in everyone and provide opportunities for this to be celebrated. Develop a creative skill amongst the staff that can then be taught to children. Display that skill as a process in the classroom (Figure 7.5).

It's important to see that creativity is a foundation for enquiry, not just an extra bit. It should permeate the school and it can only do that if it is *valued*, *celebrated* and *understood*. The enquiries that you set up should have lots of opportunities to recognise these creative stages. How can you promote creativity so that everyone values it? You have to show that it links together and has a purpose for the future. Expressing ideas and thoughts creatively, through art, music or dance, separates us from robots and to instil that in children is for them to see the grown-ups around them being creative and talking about those creative skills.

Creativity promotes those traits that we all want for our children to be lifelong learners. It develops that curiosity in experimenting and exploring and having a go at something new and helps consolidate self-identity and confidence. We need to enjoy doing and thinking about what we love, and be confident in expressing ourselves.

Be very aware of what could be blocking the creative process in your school. Is it that creativity isn't valued into children's futures? Bring outside speakers into school for children to interview or see their work in action. Find professions where creativity is needed so that it's not just viewed as

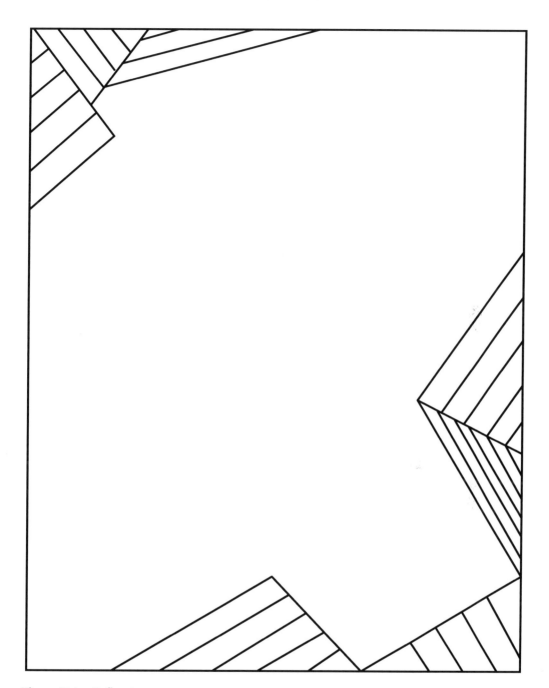

**Figure 7.4**    Reflection page

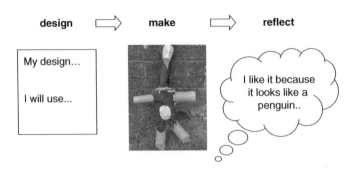

**Figure 7.5**

an art teacher skill. Creativity fits into so many professions, so go and find examples in your community. This could be an enquiry in itself, particularly, for older children who may be already thinking about what they want to study or do in the future. The children could devise a questionnaire to local businesses or organisations and find out how creativity is displayed in those professions. This again makes several links across the curriculum, and subject leaders should know this is happening. Use the reflective page (Figure 7.6) to explore creative possibilities in all environments.

By researching creativity in a profession you would be hitting many subjects, such as geography, IT and literacy skills, and this would give subject leaders lots of evidence of the impact of their subject on enquiry and learning and vice versa. Celebrate the creativity that is happening in your school either through display, 'shout-out' boards or awards. Once children realise that creativity is being praised and celebrated they will want to join in. Monitor how creativity is developing with your children and staff. Can they explain the creative process and identify the skills needed to make the creative process flourish. I can just imagine a 'creativity-off', where children explain and praise creativity amongst their peers.

Creativity needs to be understood as an integral part of enquiry. If you want an enquiry to be successful then creating ideas, to things, to new questions, is something that doesn't stand still. It's something that should be seen and referred to and shared. Creativity needs to have an audience so make sure staff and children see it and praise it. Fundamentally, we all need to see that creativity has a purpose and is relevant to learning now and in the future.

Being creative in Early Years is something you will see a lot of. From designing models of a tree house to thinking there's a fairy house at the base of the tree, young, divergent thinkers can suspend belief and imagine all sorts of different amazing ideas. They are also able to solve problems and think around questions. We found a dead fox during an expedition to the woods. Instead of the children being frightened or disgusted, they were genuinely

**Figure 7.6** Reflection page

concerned. They were intrigued as to how it had got there because it was over a fence, next to a pond. The discussion around what had happened was fascinating. They came up with many different possibilities, from it being run over to that it had become poorly. These solutions still had problems, so the level of reasoning and creativity in their thinking was high. It was a real and a genuine experience that then stimulated stories, talks about healthy eating, death and bereavement of family members. An honest chance happening that turned into a creative discussion that the children will remember for a long time. We continued the theme of health and life-cycles further and they used and applied this learning to other animals and themselves.

## Play

This definitely needs to go in your toolkit. You need to build play into the timetable from early on and don't let it disappear as the children become older. It's a crucial part of development which, again, lays the foundations for successful enquirers.

Giving children the time and space to explore resources will develop so many skills and characteristics that you would be foolish to avoid it. I sometimes have Year 6 helpers in my class at lunchtime and I let them explore the classroom. It is brilliant watching them because they access the environment meant for a 5-year-old but with 11-year-old eyes.

They adapt what is in front of them to create a game or scenario which is relevant to them. So I've seen a 'physical development' game of tweezering lids from a water tray into a tub evolve into a whole new level of activity, with rules, targets, estimations and rewards. Whatever age the child is, time should be allocated to develop this playful nature.

The view of play at times can be negative, so it's about presenting it as an enquiry skill that goes hand-in-hand with questioning, creativity and all the other skills in your toolkit.

To know that children are happy to imagine, create and challenge themselves as well as interact and be sociable has to be a good thing. Playing matters in the early years and it should continue to matter as learners into the future. As adults, if we get a new phone or TV we like to play around with it first to establish how easy it is to use or what it can do. If you start a new gym class, then usually you have a taster session – a 'play' session to make sure you're going to enjoy it, or you're not going to break your neck on the treadmill!

So, play should again be recognised as an integral part of 'winging it'. It's like the rehearsal before the main event and the more practised you are at it, the more confident you will become.

After a recent enquiry day at school, I asked the staff to reflect on the best bit of the day and suggest an area of development for the next one. There was an overwhelming feeling from most year groups that they needed to provide more play-based opportunities. They had hooked the children in with engaging stimulus, but the activities were too adult intensive. This was the feedback from Reception up to Years 5 and 6. The staff had prepared amazing opportunities, but they were exhausted.

Next time our aim is to introduce some play activity, either based around drama or investigations, but with an element of playfulness and freedom to explore without an adult overseeing, modelling or directing. What a great opportunity for all children to collaborate and enjoy exploring without someone expecting objectives, asking continuous questions or pressing for an outcome. Everybody made it their mission to include this in the enquiries next time. It doesn't just mean that the children have the opportunity to play. You need to do it too. You need to feel what it's like to explore and be playful.

In Early Years, we often leave a resource out and wait to see what happens, or the adult will start playing a game and wait and see who joins in or who interacts. This approach gives you a lot of information about how imaginative, creative and playful a child is. It also highlights who is good at leading play, generating storylines or solving issues. Wouldn't it be amazing if older children were allowed the freedom to see you play and join in with you, lead you, listen to you and make a playful connection?

Once you have done this and felt how skilled children are at playing, it opens up possibilities of future teaching or modelling. Older children become a bit more cynical if they've not had the enquiry skills explained within their experiences, so when you bring out a treasure map that you (allegedly) found on the beach they are dismissive of it being real. This can then dictate how the session will go, whereas if they've experienced lots of play-based learning they will be accustomed to it and be welcoming to the notion of pretending.

My girls at home, up to the age of about 7, would say, "We're 'tending!" Whenever I heard this I knew that something really special was happening. "I'm 'tending I'm a mermaid." Or "you 'tend you're a dolphin." They were allowing themselves to direct their own play and talk about what they were being, or doing and going off into an imaginary world. It was magical to watch and listen to and I'm sure it was the foundations for them to become successful readers and writers.

In a world where many children, throughout the primary school years, stay indoors and 'gaming' is on the rise, it's almost as if they have lost the skill of playing. Many are reliant on other things or people to provide their entertainment.

We need to bring play back into the experiences of all our children. Early Years settings are providing bucketloads of playful experiences, from pretending to be pirates to squashing clay and making sausages. This should be extended right through the primary phase so that older children retain that ability to pretend and make-believe to become resilient in creating and imagining their own entertainment and be self-reliant as a playful learner. The play would evolve, mature and progress into more involved narratives or complicated parts, but in order to arrive at this the playful groundwork needs to be maintained. You need to continue the playful skill in your toolkit (Figure 7.7).

When you're playing you are making tiny decisions and choices as you go. You are listening and speaking about preferences and taking on roles and responsibilities in a safe and happy situation. Without really knowing it, you are practising all those basic curriculum skills which will later underpin how you learn. Use the reflection page (Figure 7.8) to note down possible play opportunities.

## Skills progression

When a teacher is actively engaged in an enquiry or any lesson, many are naturally prepared for the progression of the skills on display. They probably know instinctively how to support and challenge the children in front of them. They will also know what skills are needed before an objective is covered and what questioning is necessary to either support or extend learning. It will be identified by planning as differentiation or progression. Many teachers instinctively know this and can adapt their interaction and challenges. It would be useful for all staff to regularly discuss this progression to ensure everyone is aware of the stages and steps they are teaching.

Subject leaders may have already provided skill progression through the primary phase, so use these to ensure all staff have access to and awareness of them. Newly or recently qualified teachers may need guidance with this as well as teaching assistants and students on teaching placements. You could provide cue cards with the skills progression on them for the relevant enquiry. This would support less confident staff to know what questions to ask if a child needed support. They could instantly see the steps needed in order to be successful when working on an objective and equally, at a glance know what to look for if a child needs pushing to a greater depth.

These cue cards need to be referred to on the enquiry planning with desired objectives to be explored along with the activity, so that whoever is supporting that enquiry has the skill progression tool ready to be used. Less confident staff need to discuss with their team how to implement this skill progression, especially if you are aiming to explore skills that aren't obviously subject based, for example in teamwork or presenting a news report. You need to

| What comes before? | Year 1 Art skill example | What comes next? |
|---|---|---|
| Find and talk about favourite things in their own and other's work. | Describe what they think about the work of others. | Express clear preferences and give some reasons. (E.g. I like this because…) |

**Figure 7.7**   Skills progression grid example

think carefully about what goes before this activity and how you can extend it (Figure 7.9). In doing this, you are making the learning personal to individuals and tailored to their needs.

It will become clear to less confident teachers the steps they need to follow in order to create a successful enquiry. It will also help to ease those teachers who are not fully on board with enquiry to realise curriculum objectives are still relevant to enquiry; that it's not the content of skills that needs changing but the way in which the skills are delivered.

## Back-up plan

You now have a toolkit to help you engage with enquiries and practice 'winging it'. But there's one more thing to put in: your back-up plan. On the planning grid, you need to put down a few ideas in case things don't go to plan. Hopefully, you will have checked resources to make sure that all is in order and the staff involved know what they're doing. You've also sent letters out to parents if costumes or things from home are needed and everyone is aware of changes to timetables and/or venues.

I can't possibly think of any other thing that would cause you to abandon an enquiry but just be prepared to discuss a few scenarios with your team so that everyone feels prepared if last-minute changes occur. The notion of 'winging it' should change to a more positive feel. Many will say that they are 'winging it' all the time in their professional and personal life, though it is portrayed in a negative way. You actually have to be quite skilled in let-ting go and to see it as a choice rather than a response. Yes … you are being pro-active!

Having a back-up plan isn't just about having physical things ready just in case. Some teachers have a few activities up their sleeves on the off-chance that they are put on the spot and have to produce something in min-utes. I think we all have this skill; it just needs nurturing and viewing in a

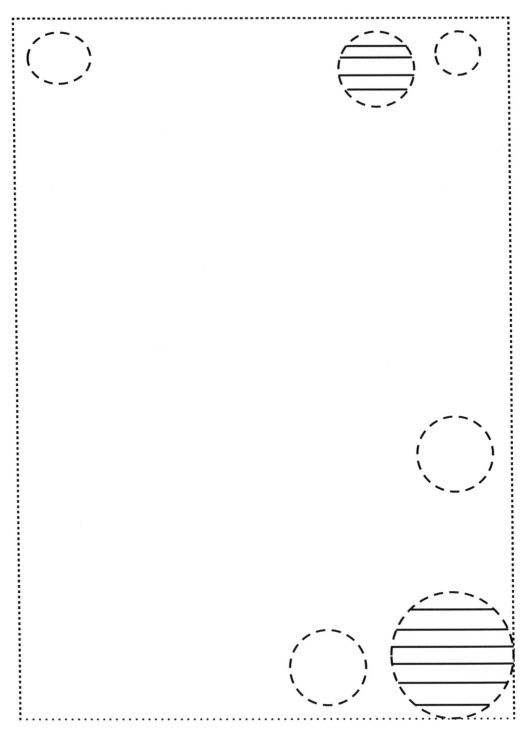

**Figure 7.8** Reflection page

**Figure 7.9**    Reflection page

different way. Newly qualified or recently qualified teachers and students on placements will need to have a few lesson ideas or circle time games in their toolkit in case the intended learning hasn't quite happened, or a child has an amazing idea and you decide to run with it. A back-up plan is also a state of mind in being flexible to situations, adapting to events and having the confidence to steer an out-of-control idea to bring it back on course.

I remember doing an investigation into plants with Year 2 children many years ago and it was being observed by other staff. I wanted the children to tell me the conditions that plants need in order to grow and sequence the stages of growth, and to name plant parts. Something that I thought would last 20 minutes or so lasted only 6! What was I going to do? Also, I was being observed! Luckily we had packets of seeds and soil, etc. outside ready for planting in the garden. I was an inexperienced teacher who should have thought about starting this lesson with the children handling seeds, pots and soil. But, 'younger teacher' me chose to go straight in with the theory. Having the resources nearby and adapting their use, looking back, was me using a back-up plan.

The children knew the facts and theory mainly because back then, it was being taught in every year group, as well as in nurseries and pre-school. So, the children needed to access this knowledge and enquiry at a much higher level. My back-up plan had to cater for most children having strong prior learning and so needed to be challenging. Easy, they know the facts but had never actually done the planting or choosing best spots for planting by reading the advice on the packets. The planting had previously been modelled and plants had been presented as diagrams. Real-life experience of reading instructions from real objects and handling real plants and soil became a much more genuine learning experience. Something those children will remember.

Another example of a back-up plan was when I was expecting an Ofsted Inspector to watch my dance lesson. It was in the days when you had a warning. The lesson ended with no inspector and we walked back up the corridor dejected. As we entered the classroom he was sitting waiting for our return. "Ah, I can't wait to watch your poetry session" was his announcement. In a matter of seconds, I had to exercise my warmth-o-meter and back-up plan, as well as all the other tools in my toolkit. I glanced at my timetable and saw that I *had* written poetry for the end of the day and started to panic inside, although on the outside I *was* that swan. "Certainly," I said. "Let's just get everybody changed and we'll start."

On my shelf, I found a large poetry book for children, all about the senses. It turned into such a positive session. I think we all forgot that an inspector was watching. We finished with a wishes poem and I asked the children to come and whisper a wish in my ear, one at a time, before collecting their coat for home time. It transformed from disaster or panic mode to something quite beautiful. All the adults in the room gave a huge sigh of satisfaction. The back-up plan skill is the ability to be flexible and adaptable and realise the possibility of a situation.

It's the willingness to find something amazing out of a potential problem. What an amazing role model you will be if you can display this to your children and staff! Your teaching life will have some hurdles to jump over, so do it with style, grace and empathy for the viewers. If you can confidently steer a problem back on track then you are an enquiry teacher.

This and all the toolkit skills need to be articulated to the staff through a staff meeting or team discussion. Leave the toolkits image on the staffroom table and encourage regular discussion about it. Ask the question, which toolkit skill are you going to practise today? Focus on which skills are going to be important for your enquiries. Pick a tool that you think needs work on and explore how you can improve it. For example, a teacher may be inexperienced at engaging with children in a 'play' scenario and how to interject during the 'play' appropriately with questions or ideas. Don't forget that spontaneous doesn't just mean unplanned, it also means natural and relaxed, so bring out your inner 'go with the flow' vibe.

# 8

# Photo album

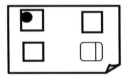

**Figure 8.1**

The album is the physical evidence that enquiry is taking place and it goes together with celebration and feedback. Quite often we get hung up on making sure the children are doing something towards an end product. If they are looking busy making something, then surely it is worthwhile! However, don't lose track of the 'unseen and intangible' skills that are of great importance to enquiry. It can take on various forms and should be appropriate to the enquiry. Maybe it will be a collection of photographs and observations to go towards a whole-school flipchart that will show evidence of questioning, writing or creativity. It could be a presentation from a group of children to the class or parents or even a 'live' recording shared on social media. Whatever it is, the photo album is the record of skills happening, which then can be used for assessment purposes, celebration or just the intrinsic knowledge that enquiry progress is taking place.

Ensuring that safeguarding measures are in place and you are following the school's policy correctly, the album can be presented however the enquirers want. It's important for children to explore a variety of ways of presenting but they need to be meaningful. Younger children will probably contribute through photographs and quotes, although as the children go through the school and become more confident and experimental in their evidence gathering, they can decide how it takes shape.

It might be worth older children documenting what they do in a diary form, similar to this book; then, the process from the beginning of an enquiry to the end can be explored. It's a very visual way of seeing the steps rather than just a finished result.

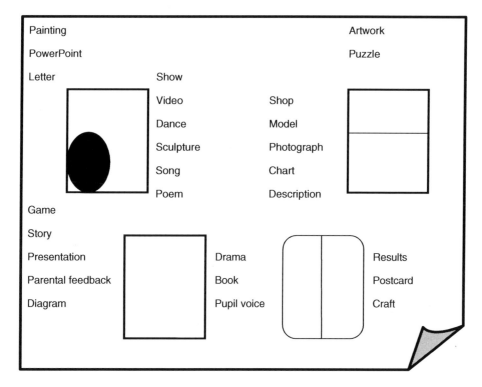

**Figure 8.2** Examples

Your photograph album could take the form of anything (see for example Figure 8.2).

The list is endless but make sure the children are involved and links are being made to the school's priorities. It's an opportunity for children to practise their presenting and publishing skills. It gives them the chance to develop their practical skills in using publishing and presenting equipment like cameras, photocopiers or CD players.

They will, more importantly, understand the need for clear voices, logical explanations and thoughtful opinions, all done in an atmosphere of warmth, celebration and respect. It's an opportunity to practise being a critic.

This is also a very good opportunity for children to receive feedback from adults and other children and to relate it to any school marking codes you may have. This will be different in many schools. Whatever your marking code or feedback procedures are, use them for enquiry too. This then strengthens all the procedures in school and creates that evidence trail, illustrating that enquiry is alive and kicking in your school and not an isolated activity that happens once a year and has no links to curriculum skills or the school's priorities.

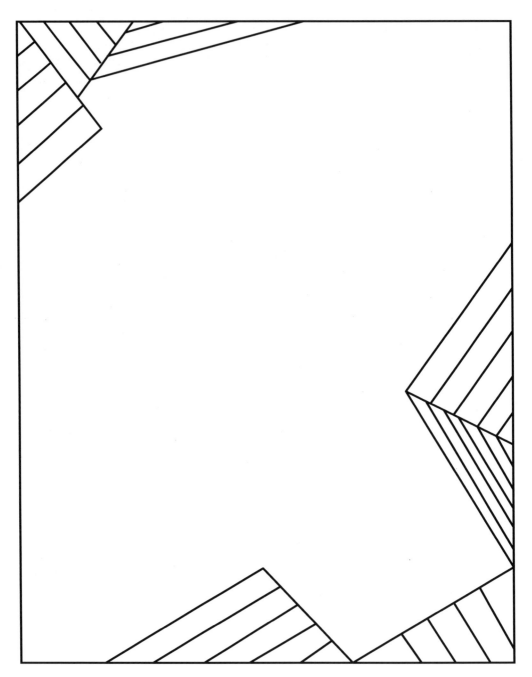

**Figure 8.3**  Reflection page

What a wasted opportunity that would be if this happened! If you want to be an enquiry school then you have to see, feel and hear those enquiry threads penetrating through everything you do and the album is the process in action. It's also a celebration of all the hard work you are doing.

The photo album has to get away from the production line mentality where every child makes the same thing, in the same way using the same things. There's nothing personal about that and it just creates stress for the adults involved, with tick lists and little creativity. Bring in an ethos that children are going to make their own decisions on how to make something or present something and allow them to have a go, make mistakes and celebrate their solutions. This will be far more memorable and rewarding in the end.

This notion of stopping the production line could end up being a priority for you once you've seen some enquiries happen. Breaking this mentality can be difficult, so look to Team Enquiry to help promote a more personalised approach. Teachers could report back during a staff meeting and discuss the benefits of personal, tailored learning approaches. If you have the opportunity to look through books, the ones that stand out are those where skills are established, where greater understanding is explored and then knowledge is applied to new contexts. This should be the same for the Photo Album. With threads of dialogue, adjustment and reflection weaving through.

It is an incredible opportunity to further strengthen all the procedures happening in school and for you to triangulate what enquiry teaching is taking place, what children are saying and what they are doing. It also develops the bond and communication with parents and the community as it will become the showcase for enquiry and further growth. Use the reflection page (Figure 8.3) to discuss end results or products that are relevant to enquiry skills. Note down how you are going to reduce or even stop the production line of work approach.

# 9

# Check-out

**Figure 9.1**

This section is the evaluation to the enquiry with the children. Just as you introduced it with a check-in, now you need to bring it all together with a check-out. Essentially this is when the children can share their findings and reflect on how the enquiry went.

It's also a quick review of the enquiry rules so that you can share what a good enquirer looks like. Give examples of good listening, thinking of ideas, teamwork and collaboration that you have spotted. Take this opportunity for other staff and children to also share those characteristics of learning that have been witnessed.

This is a chance to absorb all the enquiry activity and for children to select their best bits or share something they have learnt. Just as the check-in sets the scene, the check-out ties all the thinking from the session together.

It should link to feelings and emotions again, so that everyone can reflect on the part they played in the enquiry; how they contributed, what they learnt and how they developed as an enquirer. It needs to be as simple and as obvious as that. Try not to rush this activity, it is important; it's almost like the punctuation to the sentence that brings it all together.

Circles are a good way of checking out and whilst the circle is happening you will be reviewing all the enquiry skills and rules that the children explored along the way. It's a practical way to bring the enquiry to a conclusion and for the children to celebrate their favourite parts and be positive players in the enquiry process.

This is the ultimate team-building exercise whilst it's all fresh in their minds. Express opinions from the session then everyone will get to know each other a little better which will show their strengths and preferences and highlight the things they need to develop. With young children, this can be organised with 'smileys' or in a visual mood tracker. Even for older children a visual format to show that they achieved something will go down well. Once everyone understands their own role is crucial in working collaboratively, then team performance will improve. A check-out is time to reflect on personal development, as well as the group, class or school achievements.

It can be linked to the enquiry through a sharing of results or findings, or it can be a separate theme totally or reflections of the original check-in.

Whatever form it takes, make sure that you give time for a personal development. For example: at the beginning I thought this, but now I've changed my mind and think this ... In the recent check-out with my reception class, some had remembered the 'odd one out' and said that now they know that pandas live in China. One child said how zoos were good because they kept people safe from lions, whereas someone else said that animals should be able to run. At a basic level these children are contemplating their beliefs and opinions after hearing and finding out; all good in building self-confidence.

It's also a time to comment on who showed a 'growth mindset' and discuss the positive characteristics of learning. Maybe a school priority is resilience. The children can talk about who kept going and didn't give up. Refer back to the words generated during the staff meeting that hopefully are now displayed around the school. Did those traits like communication and creativity really happen today? Children need the platform to discuss what they look like in an enquiry and check-out is the time to reflect on how those characteristics showed themselves.

All this talk will hopefully lead to further questions and development. So collect these next steps as a class, so that during the next enquiry everyone is aware of the skills or characteristics that need to be revisited or further improved. On the planning grid, decide as a team what you think your class, year group and team need to explore more deeply.

Children are often very accomplished at telling each other how to improve, so make sure this is delivered in an atmosphere of positivity, looking to improve but not dwelling on what went wrong or what somebody didn't do. If we share our next steps and document them then as a group, class or school, we are holding accountability and ensuring that we all take responsibility to reach our goal. There have got to be common themes in everybody's next steps.

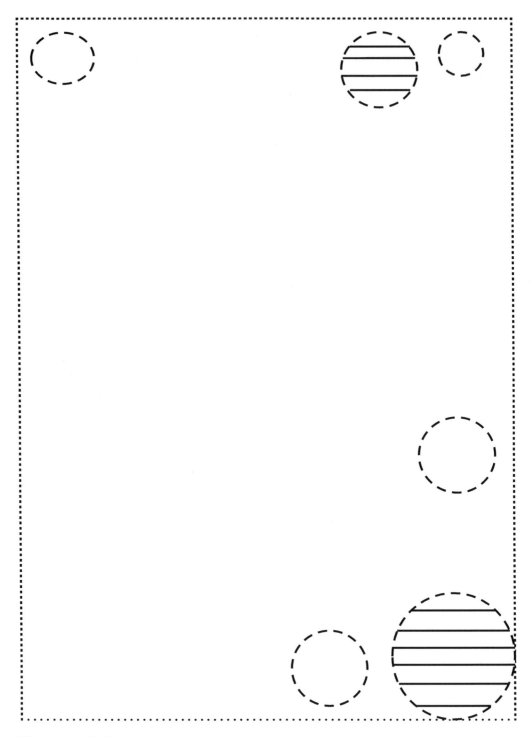

**Figure 9.2** Reflection page

Have a go on the next note page (Figure 9.2) and see if there are common themes that can be shared at staff meetings. If you are new to the school then use the check-out information to discuss with your mentor and team to ensure consistency of approach is happening in that year group. If you are an enquiry leader, build time into staff meetings to share findings. Use this knowledge to inform discussion at the next platform, 'Revisit'; it can also be combined with 'Photo album' to continue promoting enquiry skills.

# 10

# Revisit

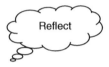

**Figure 10.1**

Now that you've seen an enquiry in action from start to finish and gathered evidence, as well as children's evaluations and reflections, you have valuable information. Remember, enquiries can last as long as they need to, so for the purposes of this book start with contained enquires which have a contained beginning, middle and end. This really allows teams to unpick each element to further inform you of staff, school or children's next steps. We will all have had quick discussions about how a lesson went or been excited to tell a colleague something they've seen on a course. These small conversations all add up to an honest and clear path to improvement and should be given the appropriate platform. On the planning grid, decide what evaluation, communication skills or other characteristics you realise need to be focussed on.

You don't have to do it straight away; sometimes it's good to leave time for learning or events to sink in. However, don't leave it too long; you don't want everyone to forget the 'buzz'. Just remember to value the responses and use them to propel the school forward. It's quite a sophisticated skill to be able to reflect honestly and use it to improve, but if it starts from an early age and becomes part of the enquiry process then it will be as valuable as creativity or collaboration. This part of the enquiry process will allow for flexibility and avoid a fixed mindset. All those tools in the enquiry toolkit from questioning strategies, language menu, warmth-o-meter, creativity, play, skills progression and back-up plan need to be in full operation to allow deep, meaningful improvement to happen. These tools that you have developed are not dominant or didactic; they are subtle, yet provide the backbone of an enquiry school. So use them and reflect on how well they've been used.

Firstly, start with pupil voice. If you can't find the time to speak to children yourself then devise a feedback/evaluation sheet for your enquirers to fill in. Younger children may need more guidance but if you can do it yourself then you will feel and digest the evaluations which will have a greater impact on you.

Figure 10.2 gives an example of pupil voice evaluation.

Add your own questions for your children that are pertinent to the stage your children are at. The enthusiasm from the enquiry needs to be captured and used to propel the children further and to make the enquiry cycle habitual, giving clarity to why they are doing it. It has to overtly show that improvements will benefit their learning. Promoting their own curiosity and creativity, as well as collaborative, social and communication skills needed now and in the future as they develop into learners for life.

Now that you have a range of responses throughout the school, you should start noticing trends and themes. Each school will be different depending on its own stage of creativity or enquiry. Now that you have the information, act on it. You need to give feedback to the staff and do it as a group. The team of teachers can discuss the themes and try to come to more solutions. For example: "I think next time I'll need to put in more play during the enquiry." "It seems that this group didn't really listen to each other, so I'm going to do more listening games during the day."

It could even be as basic as making sure everyone is doing it at the same time, so that the conversation with all the staff will diffuse your role by asking them to change when they don't want to, instead changing opinions to "this worked really well because every class was doing it at the same time in our year group and there was a tangible 'buzz' in the rooms".

At the same meeting, ask staff to fill in a teacher evaluation sheet about what worked well (Figure 10.3). A good way to do this is to ask them to think about three positives and a wish for next time. They need to discuss these with their teams so that issues can be addressed in the next enquiry.

Along with the pupil voice, this will give you evidence and also a mood tracker to see how it's going. There's an opportunity for personal growth and space to reflect on growing facilitator skills, as well as recording subject skills, ensuring that enquiry is supporting the curriculum. Subject leaders will want to know this, so in this open forum share this knowledge, examples of planning grids and 'photograph albums' from the enquiries.

The overriding feeling I got when I did this exercise was that children loved having the freedom and of being in control of the timetable. They were bursting with enthusiasm about doing things differently, dressing up and working with their friends. However, I was underwhelmed by their ideas for

**Pupil Voice – Reception**

**Did you enjoy the enquiry day? Why?**

*Yes – All They enjoyed dressing up and having face paints and being animals.*

**What activities did you do?**

*Dancing in the hall. Making a lion mask. Drumming and doing music.*

**What skills did you learn?**

*Learnt to play drums. Learnt about which animals live in Africa.*

**What would you like to do next time?**

*Dressing up*

*Football /sports*

*Skateboarding and roller skating.*

*Bring your own toy day.*

*Summer*

---

**Pupil Voice – Year 5**

**Did you enjoy the enquiry day? Why?**

*It was different. We could be creative. Make our own things.*

**What activities did you do?**

**What skills did you learn?**

*Making our own PowerPoints. Worked things out for ourselves. Research. I learnt that I am awesome on the kazoo. Good for self confidence.*

*Making our own ideas.*

**What would you like to do next time?**

*Dress up.*

*Do our own ideas.*

*Sport.*

*Science investigations and making sl*

*Natural world.*

**Figure 10.2**

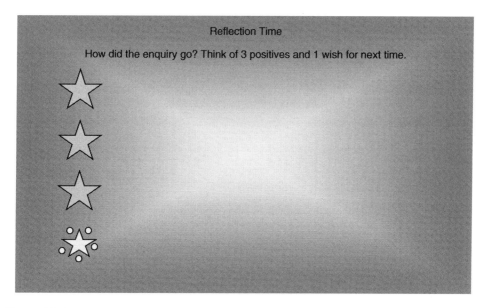

Reflection Time

How did the enquiry go? Think of 3 positives and 1 wish for next time.

**Figure 10.3**

future enquiries. I thought they'd have interesting ideas and be curious about a varied range of subjects.

The answers I collected seemed very limited. We had one idea about the natural world, wanting to explore nature. This was off the back of a previous topic about rainforests so was extended from that. There wasn't really the scope for big-picture thinking with the rest of the ideas. I was disappointed that the spark of curiosity didn't seem to be there, especially as 'engagement' had been a key focus for staff and a 'thirst for learning', a key focus for the school as a whole.

At this point, I thought that maybe my research had been too narrow, so next time I'm going to gather feedback from a wider range and maybe pin-point certain year groups. This had to be fed back to staff so that they know to include opportunities for 'big think' reasoning and imaginative thinking into the next enquiry. I know that it is happening in school, that there is a thirst for learning; it just needs to be more apparent in discussions and pupil voice.

It's such a worthwhile activity doing a learning walk – you get a real feel for what is happening on a daily basis. It's less intrusive for the teachers, and in reality it's more informative because of its informality. You can see the learning taking place and you can take stock of the environment and talk to the children about their thinking and learning. If you are an enquiry leader make time for this during 'wow' days or enquiry sessions. You will be able to tangibly see the discussions and conversations you've been having with staff in practice. It should satisfy you that enquiry is taking place and when

**Figure 10.4** Reflection page

you're explaining to the head teacher or other colleagues what enquiry looks like in your school, you will have a much clearer view along with examples to back it up.

The examples will satisfy the view of your strengths as an enquiry school and also identify areas that need to be further developed, such as more child-led planning in Key Stage 2 or more use of drama and role play as a stimulus in Year 2 for example.

This is all vital evidence to go towards the School's Development Plan also, so that subject leaders can analyse their subject impact on enquiry and the learning that is taking place and vice versa. This may become a good time for the headteacher and senior leadership team to also discuss how evaluations are impacting on the future of the school. Wouldn't it be great if enquiry skills became a theme for teacher and teaching assistant observations!

This platform gives everyone the opportunity to reflect on what has worked well and what needs to be done better. It will create a very clear action plan for the whole school to follow with themes for different phases and the whole school to act on. Once this system has been done a few times, it should become part of the enquiry cycle. Very much like the feedback systems you already have in school. Let them complement each other and use them side by side. Inform all staff of this vital process during a staff meeting. It will become second nature and be embedded in the school's learning ethos.

This is also a perfect opportunity for Team Enquiry to enthuse about what has happened during the enquiries. Try and do a 'best bits' montage and more importantly why they're viewed as 'best bits'. What happened? Why was it amazing? What happened to make you feel this way? You are doing a mood tracker for changes in opinion to enquiry.

Your Team Enquiry should also be growing in force as new ideas are shared and everyone wants a piece of the enquiry action. Without being competitive, as that can become destructive, it's about showcasing the best bits. Through modelling the positive elements to all, staff will become increasingly more confident in 'winging it'.

Any comments from feedback sessions can be noted on the reflection page (Figure 10.4) to inspire you to keep moving forward or see the gaps and to inform any future destinations.

## 11

# Bon voyage!

So, now you have all you need to make your enquiry journey meaningful and successful. You can't do it on your own; you have to try to include everyone to gain full impact. As you go along this journey you will find new skills to explore alongside the children. Uncover them, understand them and then practise them to improve your teaching and learning to the best it can become. Also, share them with colleagues to build consistency throughout the school. If you are an enquiry leader, showcase the amazing work Team Enquiry is doing.

Be that go-to person for others who want to develop their facilitating skills. Offer to watch a lesson or be the scribe for someone during an enquiry, who wants to know what they actually said or did to develop their language menu or warmth-o-meter. You are the link between learning, teaching and enquiry improvement, so strengthen yourself by providing the best enquiry experience for everyone at school and ultimately strengthen the school.

The future of education is unsure; so is the role of the teacher. In order to redefine our place in learning, we need to be totally aware of where we are, who's going with us and how we're going to get there. Especially in a time when we're not sure what education will look like in the future? We do know that enquiry should play a crucial part in equipping ourselves and learners to be active and curious enquirers of the future.

When I started my university degree, my art lecturer told me that starting this course would open my eyes to a whole new way of seeing the world: light and shape, texture, lines. This has evolved again for me now, by seeing all the enquiry skills in action around me. Spotting those layers of characteristics around school makes me hyper-aware of those learning threads and I love it!

In following this guide, those worries about letting go or going off on a tangent will no longer stay as a worry; rather, they will become an area to develop and face up to. They will no longer be a barrier but an opportunity.

Figure 11.1

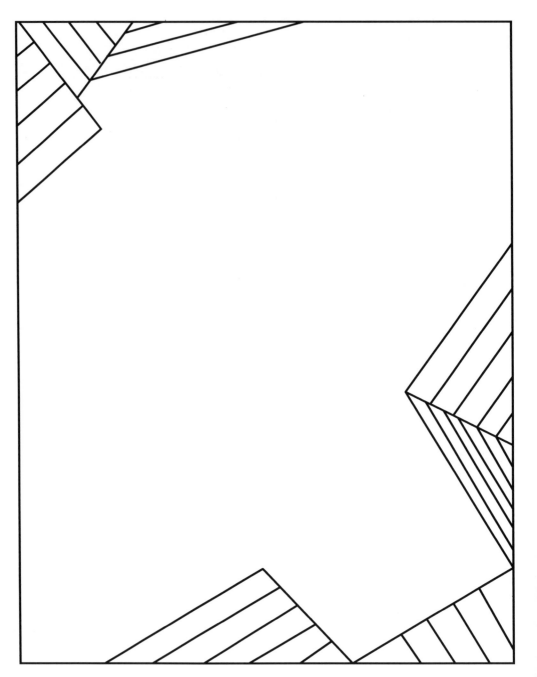

**Figure 11.2**    Reflection page

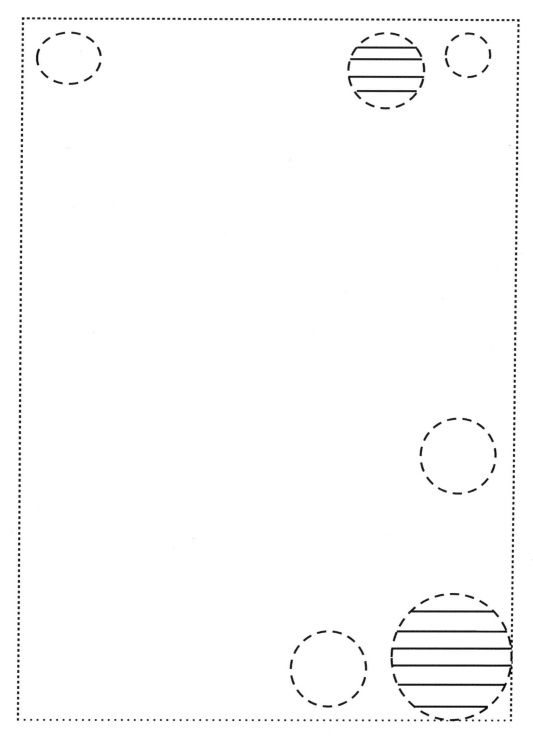

**Figure 11.3**   Reflection page

If you let something unravel, then it will. Taking control of these subtle skills that you now have in your toolkit will make you a force of nature, bringing all the learning and enquiry skills together to a clear and focussed path for yourself and your school. By now it's not just you – Team Enquiry is growing in force and together you will turn teaching and learning around.

I think we should look back at your Wanted poster in Platform 2 – 'Before you go' (Figure 11.1). Is it still the same? Look back at your notes about your qualities. Have they developed further? I think you should re-do it now that you've done all this work with your school and see how you've progressed (Figures 11.2 and 11.3). Your ability to concentrate the identification of your strengths will be greater and reference it back to the toolkit, so that you can see gaps and future endeavours.

When I first started this I thought it would take a long time and that some would sneer at my efforts. It has taken years rather than months, which to many may seem too long. But the drip effect over a longer period was needed. New staff have come on board, established staff have responded because they've seen it work and I've been on learning walks and have been blown away by the enquiry in action. I did it all following an enquiry model. I didn't go in and didactically blast my ideas to everyone. I set the enquiry model going and it gathered its own momentum, gaining ground as its value increased and the skills improved.

There's an expectation now that this is how we learn and how we teach; looking around I think we're happier for it. I couldn't have done it on my own, so this guide is one big celebration of how hard my colleagues have worked to implement my enquiry ideal. Also to the children for challenging how we teach, so that their expectations are high and ultimately, are enthusiastic and energetic to learn.

I really hope this guide will inform you and your school on how to become the best learners and enquiry teachers that you can be, so that the toolkit becomes how you teach and those deep-rooted learning experiences become a regular feature in your enquiry school.

So, good luck on this journey. I hope you will find it as fulfilling as I do in making me awake to how we learn.

# Bibliography

Bell, Stephanie (2010) *Project-based learning for the 21st century: skills for the future.* New York: Routledge, Taylor Francis Group.

Brand, Williem (2017) *Visual thinking: empowering people and organizations through visual collaboration.* Amsterdam: BIS Publishers.

Berliner, Wendy and Eyre, Deborah (2018) *Great minds and how to grow them: high performance learning.* New York: Routledge, Taylor and Francis Group.

Ephgrave, Anna (2018) *Planning in the moment with young children: a practical guide for practitioners and parents* (a David Fulton book). London: Routledge, Taylor and Francis Group.

Jesson, Jill (2012) *Developing creativity in the primary school.* Maidenhead, UK: Open University Press.

Kleon, Austin (2014) *Show your work! 10 ways to share your creativity and get discovered.* New York: Workman publishing company.

Robinson, Sir Kenneth (2010) *Changing education paradigms. RSA Animate..* Available at: https://www.bing.com/videos/search?q+changinh+education+paradigms+sir+ken+robinson&view=detail&mid=775EDF829E4B8B284A1C775EDF829E4B8BT84A1C&FORM=VIRE.

Murdoch, Kath (2015) *The power of inquiry: teaching and learning with curiosity, creativity and purpose in the contemporary classroom.* Melbourne, Australia: Seaster Education.

Patton, Alec (2012) *Work that matters.* London: Paul Hamlyn Foundation.

Thomas, Ulrika (2000) High Tech High. Available at: https://wwwhightechhigh.org/.

Trueman, Lynda *Early excellence: Centre for inspirational learning.* Available at: earlyexcellence.com.

Webb, Rosemary (2006) *Changing teaching and learning in the primary school.* Maidenhead, UK: Open University Press, McGraw-Hill Education.

Whitaker, Todd (2010) *Leading school change: 9 strategies to bring everybody on board.* Larchmont, NY: Eye on education.

# Index

Printed in Great Britain
by Amazon